Sales On The Line

SALES
ON THE LINE

MEETING THE BUSINESS DEMANDS OF THE '90s THROUGH PHONE PARTNERING

Sharon Drew Morgen

Metamorphous Press
Portland, Oregon

Published by

Metamorphous Press
P.O. Box 10616
Portland, Oregon 97210-0616

Copyright © 1993 by Sharon Drew Morgen
Editorial and Art Direction by Lori Stephens
Printed in the United States of America

Morgen, Sharon Drew, 1946-
Sales on the line : meeting the business demands of the '90s
through phone partnering / Sharon Drew Morgen ;
foreword by Larry Wilson ; preface by Robert Dilts.
p. cm.
Includes index.
ISBN 1-55552-047-2
1. Telephone selling. 2. Telemarketing. 3. Telephone in
business. 4. Oral communication. I. Title.
HF5438.3.M67   1993
658.8'4--dc20   93-7812

Contents

SECTION TWO—THE HOWS

SECTION THREE—THE APPLICATION

This book is dedicated to
Jackie, Claire, Jane, Peter, and Ben
who never stopped believing in me.

Author's Note

This book is divided into three sections: **The Whys, The Hows, and The Application.**

If you would like an immediate view of the sales, prospecting, qualifying, customer service, and problem-solving skills you will possess by the end of the book, I invite you to read the Applications section first. However, because of the paradigm shift in the presentation of questioning and listening, rapport- and relationship-building, and "sales" versus "buying facilitation," I request that you read the other sections as well.

To take into account the two genders, I have alternated chapters between the feminine and masculine pronouns.

SALES ON THE LINE

Acknowledgments

Where does an idea come from? Rupert Sheldrake says it's the collective unconscious. That is certainly possible, for there is nothing new or undiscovered in these pages: it's all been thought of, felt, practiced, and recognized before. And yet without the ideas and commitment of a few people, the language to transmit the ideas—given the methods and structure I've used—would have precluded the writing.

In 1984, I first heard the phrase, **the map is not the territory**. These words changed my life. To believe that every person operates out of his/her own value system, equally valid and equally personally effective as mine, was mind-boggling. Until then, I had judged people according to my own standards, making the world a place where "right" and "wrong" built the structure through which to make decisions.

But the understanding that each one of us had our own "rights" and "wrongs," that no one of us had the market on either, gave me a new world to discover. How could I make sense of the person in front of me if we viewed the world through different filters? I needed to find the means to set aside pre-existing beliefs and discover a way to access another person's patterns.

I set about studying NeuroLinguistic Programming (NLP) in England, where I was living. Gene Early was my teacher through three certification programs. Through him, I learned that information transmission was possible in a learning environment filled with respect for individual differences. He followed the teachings of John Grinder and Richard Bandler, the original thinkers and initiators of NLP. I owe a great debt to these three men who laid the groundwork and the structure of the ideas presented in this book.

Along the way I met Robert Dilts. With his heart leading the way, Robert has taken NLP and advanced it into exciting and innovative areas: the modeling of people and leadership skills in big business; the promotion of beliefs as part of health; the study and breakdown of creativity; and the structure of learning. It is Robert, more than anyone, who taught me how necessary it is to bring relationship, respect, and integrity into every communication. It is with honor I thank him.

I also owe thanks to the NLP trainers, authors, and associates I have learned from during the years: Eileen Watkins-Seymour, Graham Dawes, David Gordon, Dot Feldman, Steve Andreas, Judith DeLozier, Barbara Whitney, and Genie Laborde. I also owe John Grinder another acknowledgment for giving me a model of how to use my intuition as a way of connecting with the underlying meaning of another's communication.

It is also vital for me to express my appreciation for the town of Taos, New Mexico, which provided me a gentle resting place to discover how my heart and my business visions could interact.

One more note of thanks must go to my parents, Gert and Marty Feingold. They provided me a special opportunity to seek the structure of communication in order to make sense of my world. Without them, my lifelong search for clear, respectful communication may not have taken place.

I appreciate the time you are taking to read this book. Hopefully, there are many of us who are dedicated to changing the business world as it exists today in order to create a new paradigm which puts people first. I hope you enjoy my map.

Sharon Drew Morgen

Preface

Sharon Drew Morgen's *Sales On The Line* makes as much of a contribution to the field of NeuroLinguistic Programming as it does to the profession of sales. Sharon Drew has written a passionate, intelligent, and very practical book about how to apply both fundamental and leading-edge NLP skills to effective telephone sales. This is one of those special books that has as much value for an advanced NLP practitioner or novice as it does for a salesperson unfamiliar with NLP, who would like some simple and pragmatic tips on how to be more successful.

Sharon has tapped into the most effective (and least manipulative) contributions of NLP. In fact, her book demonstrates beyond a doubt that the most significant contribution of NLP to the area of sales and marketing is not in manipulating people but in facilitating effective relationships. The underlying message of her book is that it is possible to get to know and respect your client's model of the world and still achieve your own personal goals—the trick is to have the necessary skills to enter and then enrich another person's world view (and learn something about your own along the way).

This book provides a lot of very practical skills with which to respect and manage diversity and yet still successfully reach one's sales goals. It is clear that Sharon Drew is dedicated to her subject and knows it thoroughly. Her book is filled with tips, anecdotes, examples, and exercises as well as a strong theoretical structure. She is able to guide the reader effortlessly between theory and practice. I am especially impressed with the way Sharon Drew has managed to incorporate both multiple levels of communication and multiple perspectives into some very simple but effective techniques for improving listening skills and asking questions.

Having been one of Sharon's teachers as well as a colleague, I feel a sense of pride as well as appreciation about her work. She has not come by her knowledge and success by magic but has earned it through her dedication and intelligence. "Learn" is the word "earn" with an "l" in front of it. I think Sharon Drew would agree with me that this "l" is for "listening."

Robert Dilts
The Dynamic Learning Center
Santa Cruz, California
November, 1992

Foreword

The telephone. It has always been there, occupying a small corner of your desk. Now it's also in your car, hanging from your belt, and soon, no doubt, it will be surgically implanted.

Yet the ubiquitous telephone, and its evil twin, Voice Mail, are probably the most misunderstood and most underutilized instruments in business today. In the near future, the telephone will become the critical tool for anyone who wants to survive and thrive in the ongoing business revolution. The ability to use the telephone as the primary means of communication will make all the difference for many businesspeople.

Of course, you ask, "Everybody uses the telephone, every hour of every day—so what's the big deal?"

But what if . . .

Your revenue production were completely dependent on that box on your desk?

What if the costs of a face-to-face sales call were so astronomically high that "face-to-face" selling simply wasn't done anymore?

What if your only contact with your customers was by phone?

What if you went to see only those prospects who were ready to close?

That's the future for many of us, and that is why Sharon Drew Morgen's book, *Sales On The Line*, is so important.

If you're thinking, "That could never happen to me," read on. First, some context. Let's talk about business today. Recently I asked a vice-president for consumer sales at US West, an intelligent, articulate woman, to describe business today. She responded with just one word: "Chaos."

Chaos means total disorder, which aptly describes not only the large game of business but, more to the point, the world of sales today.

In *Partnering: Creating Customers For Life,* a business program we facilitate at the Pecos River Learning Centers in Santa Fe, New Mexico, we have had the good fortune to learn first-hand from participants ranging from CEO's to salespeople about what is changing in their industries and markets and in their relationships with customers.

What we've heard has echoed from industry to industry:

Exponential increases in competition from global sources have created many more choices for customers among products and services that basically look alike. (It's like a supermarket out there!) More choices produce fickle customers who will jump ship on a whim, for a price break, for a toaster.

Fickle customers with lots of choices result in huge downward pressures on prices and, more importantly, on margins and profits—the lifeblood of companies.

At the same time, we are dealing with the most sophisticated, knowledgeable group of customers in history. They are, in many ways, better at buying than most salespeople are at selling. In more and more industries, the old step-by-step sales process that guided many a salesperson home to port is no longer driven by the salesperson. It is driven by the buyer.

As a colleague of ours remarked, "The truth is that no one can sell anyone anything anymore—customers choose to buy or not to buy." Believe me, that's a major difference from the way things used to be.

As if this wasn't enough, the price of traditional selling is skyrocketing. The cost of a face-to-face sales call is measured in hundreds of dollars. The average cost of a salesperson, according to a recent study, is four times his or her base pay.

The foundation of the traditional edifice called "sales" is shaking and cracking. All over the business landscape, companies are looking for new ways to develop long-term relationships with their customers while at the same time driving cost out of the sales system.

Oddly enough—and occasionally the world works in serendipitous ways—your customers and mine are looking for the same solutions from the point of view of buying. Their worlds have gone topsy-turvey; their companies have cut layers of management and placed new expectations of "more for less" on the survivors.

These individuals no longer have the time to deal with the face-to-face sales call, whether it be a sales rep calling on them for the first time or a two-hour lunch with an existing supplier. Today, lunch is eaten at the desk, and productivity is measured in minutes rather than hours.

The solution? The telephone. The average phone transaction lasts five to seven minutes. How long does the average face-to-face sales call take? With the phone, the buyer is in control, has more flexibility in scheduling, and can get all the necessary information. Moreover, he or she can ask you to fax further details in just a few minutes.

This trend is not a flash in the pan. Major U.S. companies, including Hewlett-Packard, General Electric and IBM, are creating entirely new departments that sell and service everything over the phone.

Is this trend going to continue? Yes. In the future, the business world will be linked up electronically in ways that we cannot even yet imagine. My US West friend told me that the market her company is after is the market now served by the airlines. Their point is, why fly, why travel, why go face-to-face, when it is so much less expensive and more productive for everyone involved to do it electronically?

So, once again, technology is pushing us in new directions. How can we best use that technology? This is where *Sales On The Line* is invaluable. For years, "telemarketing" has stressed the 15-second canned presentation, in which the seller didn't dare stop talking for fear that the prospect might ask a question. Telemarketing meant "dialing and smiling," making as many calls as possible each day with the same presentation and the same speech.

Sharon Drew Morgen's *Sales On The Line* moves doing business out of the Dark Ages and into the future where customers are in control and selling means facilitating rather than manipulating. Morgen takes the reader through a "how-to" process of creating relationships over the telephone, relationships built on respect and on discovering the needs of each customer rather than attempting to force preconceived solutions.

Whether you are a salesperson or a CEO, the skills in *Sales On The Line* will be invaluable as you face this new marketplace, this new world of technology, competition and demanding customers. The future offers enormous opportunities for those who learn to use new tools and to optimize their use of old tools.

Sales On The Line provides that essential understanding and teaches those vital skills. A helpful hint: this is not a theoretical book to be skimmed and then shelved. Rather, it is a practical book which belongs right next to your telephone. Use it, practice it, and enjoy.

Larry Wilson
Pecos River Learning Centers
Santa Fe, New Mexico

Introduction

Salesperson: Hi! Mrs. Williams?
Customer: This is *Margaret* Williams.
Salesperson: How are you this evening? My name is John Smith and I'm calling to tell you about our new magazines, Mrs. Williams. Today we are making a special subscription offer available to you. If you purchase three magazines today, Mrs. Williams, we'll send you . . . All you have to do, Mrs. Williams, is make three easy payments. Can I read the list to you, Mrs. Williams?
Customer: No, thank you. Goodbye.

Does this conversation sound familiar? Can you hear what went wrong?

Salesperson: Hi! Mr. Atkins. How are *you* today?
Customer: Fine. Who is this?
Salesperson: Susan Jones from General Life. This month, we're introducing a new life insurance policy. I'm going to be in your neighborhood next Thursday from 2:00 to 4:00. Can I drop by and explain it to you?

How does this saleswoman know this customer is qualified? Will the face-to-face visit result in a buying opportunity? Or will it be another wasted trip? How much time might this salesperson waste each month visiting unqualified prospects?

Salesperson: Hi, Gwen. This is Richard.
Customer: Hi, Richard. What's up?
Salesperson: We have a problem. We won't be able to get your order to you until sometime next month. I'll call you in a few weeks with the new date, okay?
Customer: What do you *mean* you can't get it to me until next month? Do you have any *idea* what this does to me?
Salesperson: We had a problem at the plant. There's nothing I can do about it. I'll call you when I can. Sorry.

What about the customer here? What happens to a business relationship when the client's needs are not acknowledged? How could this conversation have been different if the customer, rather than the task, were put first?

When I begin a sales seminar, I ask the participants:
"When you approach a prospect or client, do you want to make a sale or do you want someone to buy?" *There is a difference.* One approach is about the sellers's needs, one the buyer's. But without a buyer, there is no sale.

For years, salespeople have been taught better ways to sell—approaches, methodologies, closes—all techniques to convince another person that we know more than she does, that she should listen to us and put her trust and money with our products and services. When your needs as a seller come first and you are simply doing the **task** of selling, sales becomes a "numbers game": you can get about 4% of the people you contact to buy from you.

However, if you get into rapport with your prospect and work from a **relationship** base, I estimate you can interest about 30% of your prospects and close 10-12%. **That's a potential increase of 300%!**

With the techniques presented in *Sales On The Line*, you'll gain the valuable skills you need to create relationships and rapport over the phone. You will learn how to help your client or prospect discover her needs *separate from your needs as a salesperson.* You will discover how to build an environment—even with a complete stranger—in which she can recognize the components of her present environment, envisage the needs of a future environment, and determine the resources she'll need to get there.

These rapport-building techniques can work to turn your prospects into satisfied clients and create a solid, supportive base with your present clients.

The methods in this book are not manipulative. *Sales On The Line* will teach you how to be a *buying facilitator,* to take control of the conversation while putting control of the buying into your customer's hands.

In the chapters ahead, the skills that support successful selling and relationship-building on the phone are broken down into their components and detailed, and you will learn specifically:

- how conversations work
- how to use your voice to create and maintain rapport
- when to speak and when to listen
- what questions to ask and when
- how to control the structure of the call to give the customer control of the content
- how to know what information you need to assist your client
- how to listen and create more effective listening patterns
- what to say when it's time to talk about your product or service
- how to help the customer see where she is, where she wants to go, and how to get there
- what internal questions will help you translate what the customer is really saying.

A special chapter on time management and structuring your work week to maximize your calling time is also included.

As I developed from a learner to a successful business woman,

I achieved financial and personal success and entered a whole new world of possibilities. By taking you through my experiences, I hope to build a relationship with you which will expand the parameters of your daily business, and your career. I'm pleased to be working with you to discover new beliefs of what's possible.

Section One

The Whys

Setting
The
Parameters

Chapter

1

Following four years of successful phone selling on Wall Street, I went to England and found myself in the unique position of starting up a group involved in the computer service field while knowing nothing about computers. I did, however, have a highly valued criterion about ensuring that customers got what they needed. I knew how to use the phone to be comfortable and in rapport with prospective clients. I led them through a questioning process—a type of funneling procedure—bringing them from the general to the specific, from what they knew to what they found to be missing. I didn't have to have any answers, since the questioning process uncovered the answers. All I had to do was supply the product which provided the solution.

My business grew from a one-woman show to forty-three people in three offices in two countries and $5 million in revenue by the fourth year. I personally brought in forty percent of the sales while performing all the duties of a company president. And I sold, created, and maintained the business using the telephone.

Doing business on the phone makes and saves money. It saves the unnecessary travel time and expense of going to unqualified prospects. Your new-found time can be used making more cold/referral calls, starting new relationships, and building them on the phone. Visits can be used to demonstrate a product, sign a contract, or just say "hello". Your time can be managed to allow for 120 calls a week (sixty cold or referral calls, thirty service calls and thirty follow-up calls), with two days for in-person visits. Imagine how your business can change and grow with 250 cold and referral calls and 250 follow-up and service calls a month—calls which can qualify a potential customer in minutes, close without a visit (if your product or service allows for it), and create and maintain long-term, loyal business relationships in which customers will buy and refer. It all can be done on the phone, and yet for years we have been trained to make face-to-face visits.

The Statistics of Communication

I have heard it said that we actually spend eighty percent of our waking moments communicating with others. Thirty percent of our communication is **talking**, while **listening** is said to be forty-five percent. Although our hearing and listening skills are taken for granted, the quality of all our relationships and effectiveness at work hinges on our ability to listen. Yet within one hour after the average person listens to a conversation, it is estimated that one-half of the specific information discussed is forgotten. Much of the rest is forgotten within eight hours, and almost all within a day. We do, however, retain the feel of a conversation or phone call—if it's friendly or hostile, for example—as well as a general recollection of what the exchange was about.

Most of us believe ourselves to be more comfortable in our visual mode for good reason. Fifty-five percent of all communication is based on non-verbal clues, such as facial expression and body language. Voice intonation—tone, tempo, pitch, cadence, and volume—makes up thirty-eight percent of our communication, while only seven percent comes from the actual words. So it seems we can gather more information quicker by talking with someone face-to-face than by making contact over the phone.

But is the eye more efficient than the ear? The research of J.J. Gibson (1904-1979) into perceptual psychology has brought out some interesting information. He found that sense organs transmit to the brain information about the stable characteristics of the environment—not meaningless patterns of sensations. The changes that occur as the organism interacts with the environment contain crucial data for perception. "Perception involves isolating *information about the form of objects,* not the form of sensory sensations." (*Pavlov's Heirs,* Steven Schwartz, 1987, pp. 80-81.) Therefore, the same amount of information is available to us whether we use visual or auditory senses to interpret them. And yet, in America, we're taught early on to trust what we see before what we hear.

Since becoming proficient at interpreting voices, I can gather far more accurate information on the phone than in person, where I can get confused with the many visual signals I receive. I get great clarity of meaning through the tone, tempo, and cadence of voices, in addition to the actual words used. I can be fooled into trusting information which is given to me in person far more easily than on the phone.

The Framework

In order to make optimal use of this book, it will be important that you understand the presuppositions and beliefs I am working from. I have found that by acting *as if* my beliefs are were true, I take more responsibility for my communication. These presuppositions fall into two categories: communications and sales.

We Are Responsible For The Outcomes
Of Our Communication

Although many of us like to blame others for not getting what we want, if we can accept the responsibility for creating the conversation we want, we can have some control over the outcome. *Whoever wants something from an interaction assumes responsibility for creating the environment which produces success.* If I make an unsuccessful call, I create the environment within which it happens. Equally so for a successful one. That means that there are no "bad" or "impossible clients," only situations to be worked out using appropriate choices.

That was hard for me to accept; for a long time I blamed my phone partner for not "getting" what I wanted him to "get." If one of us was wrong, it was obviously not I. When I began to take the responsibility for creatively going after what I wanted by using the information afforded me by my phone partner's signals, I began to really have control of my calls.

I work from the belief that *the meaning of the communication is the response it elicits, independent of the intent of the speaker.* This book will teach you how to create the specific, unique environment needed to give you the level of conversation you want from your phone partner. You can do this through conscious choice, rapport, matching, and disassociation, all topics we'll cover. And you will triple your business if you follow the suggestions and skill sets I have included.

There Is No Sale Without A Buyer

I can't count the number of salespeople who actually believe that every prospect is a potential sale. They are taught that they can CREATE a need in a client. I don't believe that. I believe that as intelligent adults we know what we need, but may not be able to access the information immediately. Think about this from your own viewpoint for a minute. Are you willing to buy every item which someone tries to sell you? Every gadget and widget pushed at you over the phone? Why should everyone else be available for your product or service?

I see the role of the salesperson as the facilitator. *It is our job to facilitate the process in which a client can discover for himself his own needs.* While it is not true that every prospect is a potential client, it is true that every prospect is a potential *relationship*. Through respect and rapport, we can build a relationship that puts the control of the sale back into its intended jurisdiction—with the buyer.

Focus on Relationships, Not Tasks

We are in the "people business" now.

Whether it's talking on the phone, selling, or customer service, we've been taught to take our job as a task, work to be done. The emphasis in the '90s, however, is on relationships. People.

I've heard it said in interviews, business magazines, and television talk shows that the companies not in the "people business" won't be around beyond this decade. Therefore, the emphasis is no longer on what we sell, but on how we relate to our customers and potential customers. I recently worked with a Fortune 500 company that had great difficulty with a reorganization. They went about creating change and chaos in what appeared to be a very rational way at first. The problem was, they forgot to get agreement from the people involved in the change. The people at the top had a hard time understanding why there was such resentment among the staff. I asked them to define their mission statement. It described the product, the cost, and the service, in that order. I asked them how it would be different if their mission was simply that they were in the people business and happened to also produce a product. They got it. If people were first, they would never have created a reorganization without first working it through with the hundreds of people who were directly affected.

If It Works, Don't Change It

The new approaches I've included in this book are for the times when what you are doing IS NOT working. Only then do you need to make new choices—when you actually acknowledge that what you're doing isn't working and give up the expectation that you will get different results if you keep trying the same thing again or harder or better. An axiom I work from is this:

> If you always do
> what you always did,
> you always get
> what you always got.

So if it's working, continue. If not, do something different. Just know the difference between the two.

Content Versus Structure

Conversations operate on many levels. The two I work with during business conversations are the *content* (the topics actually under discussion, the story line) and the *structure* in which the conversation flows (the way voices, words, questions, silences, turn-taking, and the underlying messages are used). The content of any conversation is dependent upon the structure in which it takes place.

In this book, I will show you how to:

1. create a successful structure for your calls which will assist you in creating a winning environment; and
2. grasp the meaning behind a client's message so you can confront issues up front, before they affect your results.

It is important to note the structural differences between personal calls and business calls. When we are involved in personal discussions, whoever wants to change the topic, the mood, the length, or the balance of a conversation does so. Both participants are equally responsible for the content and the structure. But in a business conversation, the person who wants something from the call or discussion is responsible for the end result. Therefore, *you,* as the buying facilitator, *should take control of the call's structure* and give your *customer control of the content* This ensures that the customer speaks on the topics you bring up—say, furniture rather than swimsuits, company organization rather than personalities—but the customer gets to say anything he wants to within those parameters. This approach continues building the rapport and relationship by ensuring that conversation is two-way and win-win.

By using the questioning strategies presented in Chapter 6, you can retain control of the structure of a call and assist your client in discovering inconsistencies in his environment, should any exist.

Choice

We are always making the best behavioral choices available to us at any given moment, given our personal and company value systems, work and family history, and general physical and emotional state. Usually, we are unconscious of the choices being made and therefore operate randomly, out of patterns well-used in the past. We are unaware of alternate behavioral possibilities and, in fact, don't know precisely *how* we did what we did. Until and unless we are able to consciously understand and delineate our patterns of behavior, we will not be able to change them.

Without choice, behavior, communications, and the nature of business relationships become random: it works when it works, and it doesn't when it doesn't. That means you can do business only with those people with whom you are in agreement. Through a series of practical exercises in the chapters ahead, you will learn how to have behavioral choice in order to create, with your customer, whatever environment is necessary for him to discover his needs and decide if your service will be of value to him.

Through **Skill Sets**, you will learn how to break down your current phone behaviors and recognize when what you are doing is working and when it's not. I recommend you keep a log or journal for the entire group of Skill Sets in order to keep track of your progress and to go back and rework possible problem areas. These exercises are not cumulative, and each set addresses different aspects of phone work and communication. Practice the exercises that cover the areas in which you desire to become more competent.

You can achieve any level of success you wish by taking the randomness out of your behavior. It's not magic. It will happen. It just takes hard work and determination—until it becomes unconsciously competent.

Learning New Behaviors

When we examine the skills needed to give appropriate behavioral choices for a particular situation, remember that some of the time your new choices may make you uncomfortable. *And that is a necessary part of learning!* In fact, let's take a look at the four stages in the learning process:

1. **Unconscious Incompetence:** You don't know that you don't know.
2. **Conscious Incompetence:** You know that you don't know.
3. **Conscious Competence:** You know that you know.

4. **Unconscious Competence:** You don't know that you know.

Once a behavior becomes part of your regular pattern, it is unconscious again and no longer uncomfortable for you, like the process you went through when you learned to drive a car. But to get to the state of unconscious competence, you must practice the new behaviors over time and go through a state I call "conscious uncomfortable."

A note about learning these skills: sometimes it's hard to be honest with ourselves when a problem is caused by our unconscious behavior. When we are unable to break a habit we consciously wish to change, an outside source is helpful. If you are having difficulty analyzing or recognizing what you are doing, and if you want to learn something new, use a tape recorder or video to monitor your current skills. You might need a colleague to observe you. If all else fails, hire a consultant. But note the importance of knowing precisely what it is you *are* doing so that you will know when it's necessary to do something different. After all, you can't know where you are going until you know where you are.

Changing Beliefs To Change Behavior

The major belief I act from is the assumption that IF I CAN LEARN TO USE THE PHONE in a different, more beneficial way for my career and customers, SO CAN YOU. We all do it in our own unique ways, of course, but changing beliefs is the first step to changing behaviors. *New behaviors will not become integrated unless they become part of your belief system and identity.* Then, rather than just perform the new behaviors, you take them on as part of who you are. Did you ever attempt a diet? Until and unless you first see yourself as a thin person, or a healthy person, your diets will be solely about what you eat (behavior). Change your belief and your behaviors automatically change. In phone sales, you must decide to **believe** that:

- each call is about creating a rapport-based environment
- you can qualify a prospect on the phone

- your job is about people first
- questions can facilitate discovery.

You will need to use new and different skills to support your new beliefs, which may create discomfort or feelings of inadequacy around the phone. With time and practice, the new skills will eventually become unconsciously competent.

Each Person's View Of The World Is Unique

I have painfully come to the realization that the way I believe the world works is a function of my own very personal belief systems and filters. *Because I believe something to be true does not make it universal.* It merely makes it *my* belief.

Just as a map of a geographical area is not the area itself but a representation of it, our perception of what is real is only our representation of reality. A too-human trait is to further believe that since we accept something as true for us, it must be true for everyone. The hardest lesson I learned throughout my career was that every person has his own reality which is unique to him and probably different from mine—and equally valid. Yet I unconsciously hang onto the wish that everyone will think, act, and believe the way I do. It certainly would be more comfortable for me.

When I decide who is right, or ignorant, or misguided, based on my own view of the world, or *map* as it is called in Neurolinguistic Programming (NLP), I lose my ability to maintain rapport with my clients. I have had to learn to step back from my own judgements and give my colleagues and customers the respect of finding their own answers, hopefully coming to me for assistance in creating solutions when appropriate. My job is to help create the environment which will give them the ability to discover the parameters of their choices. When the sales/buying cycle works through this type of respectful relationship, loyal business relationships are created.

The following is the first Skill Set. As mentioned earlier, a new set of exercises appears in each chapter and should be used with the book to help you get from your present situation--the actual beliefs and commensurate behaviors you currently use during the sales process—to your desired goal of increased effectiveness on the phone. Use them for practice and compare them to your current skills.

This entire book models the process I advocate: provide the environment within which people can understand where they are, appreciate where they need to go, and ascertain how to negotiate the difference. By traveling through the process with me, you will be able to replicate the experience in your work at any time you choose.

Skill Set 1

Noting your current behaviors

1. Break down the percentage of time you spend listening, questioning, and speaking during a different types of phone conversations (i.e. personal, cold calls, calls to suppliers). Note the differences in the percentages. Examine why there are differences. What would shifting percentages change?
2. Begin listening to people's voices. Note differences in tempo, volume, and pitch in different people at different times in the conversation.
3. Do you ever blame your phone partner if a conversation doesn't proceed the way you want it to? Have you ever felt someone was a "jerk" because he didn't respond the way you wanted him to? What aspects of your part of the conversation might have added to that perception?
4. During a business day, note how often you decide what a customer needs and try to convince him you are right. In what percentage of time are you successful at convincing someone he is wrong and you are right?
5. Are you person- or product-oriented? Would you rather have a conversation with someone and assist him in some way, or just find out what he needs and get the job done? Under what conditions are you either? Does it change in certain circumstances?
6. How do you know when something isn't working during one of your conversations? Is it through the words? Feelings? What changes in the conversation to give you the clues? Do you ever know while it is happening, or only afterward?

7. Name one or two communication behaviors you have performed for years which have consistently given you mediocre results. Begin to break down these behaviors into their component parts (i.e., voice, attitude, questioning and listening skills, need to convince, language patterns, person or product orientation). Begin to notice if there are times you achieve different outcomes through different behaviors. Break down these behaviors also. Note any similarities or differences. Are you willing to make any behavioral shifts to get different results?

8. Do you resist change? Do you believe it's possible for you to change? Are you willing to grow—though it may mean discomfort—by changing the behaviors you may decide to change?

9. Note any personal needs around being part of a customer's solution. Are you willing to look at the possibility of changing the focus of your interaction to include facilitation rather than just convincing?

Relationship

A sale occurs when one person feels comfortable and trusting enough to buy something she needs from another. This includes strangers, colleagues and management relationships. In business, we are "selling" ourselves on a daily basis to our staff, bosses, and colleagues.

But it's impossible for someone to sell without a buyer. And it's the buyer that has the greater power, as she is the "no-sayer" as well as the one who writes the checks. Whether you sell a product or a service on the phone or in person, **your ability to set up a buying environment is what makes the sale.**

The Buying Environment

I define a buying environment as a *rapport-filled, relationship-based, interactive climate in which a person with a need gets informed support in the manner most comfortable to her, regardless of the outcome of the interaction.* Remember, a buyer can "buy into" a relationship with you without even buying your product. I have often been delightedly surprised to find that an inappropriate prospect has gone out of her way to make a referral or send a note or article on just the strength of a cold call!

I'm always amazed at the number of programs which advocate myriads of approaches to selling: structured selling, programmed selling, strategic selling, systematized methodologies,
various approaches to "closing" techniques, etc. As a new salesperson, I was taught to find creative ways to get my prospective
buyer to listen to me so I could get just a few moments to pitch my
product. I was given course after course on how to handle
objections, create great opening lines, and get the buyer "warm"
by first sending a letter, note, or promotion piece. No one taught
me, however, how to call a person and find out who she was and
what her needs were by asking appropriate questions and listening to what she had to say. I was supposed to do all the talking,
while my customers did all the listening. What I didn't know then
was that the listener (who is also the questioner) has control of
any conversation as she is the one who has the most flexibility.

I believe that selling and buying come from relationship,
rather than approach, or even product knowledge. When I was
a broker at Merrill Lynch, Fenner, and Smith, I couldn't stop
opening accounts, although I was a new broker and actually told
people I didn't know what I was doing. "Neither does anyone
else," was the frequent response. "At least you are honest, and we
can have fun together." I was setting up an environment where
there was rapport, fun, and trust.

In 1979, Merrill Lynch did a study and found that the number
one reason for a customer to choose a broker was that she liked
the person. Honesty and trust came next. Last on the list was the
ability to make money. In other words, relationship was the main
criteria in three out of four categories.

In the sales business, even though we might be primarily
task- or product-oriented, we work through relationships by
definition. In my computer support business, I used to call the
technical people who worked for me "pizza programmers"
because they worked in a closed cubicle, and when it was time to
eat they had their food "put under the door" so as not to disturb
them. They were task-oriented and had no need for relationships
with anything but their computers. Salespeople don't have that
option; they must work through people and put relationships
first. When salespeople work at selling a product rather than a

person, they seek a solution to sell into and emphasize the content of the problem rather than the person in the problem. In other words, they put task ahead of relationship.

The "We Space"

A buying environment demands a comfort zone to establish trust and rapport. Have you ever purchased something from someone who made you feel uncomfortable? Probably not often, if ever. I am currently driving a car I dislike because a salesman at one dealership stepped on all of my criteria around communication and rapport. I was so unnerved by our interactions, I went across the street and bought a different make of car.

For each selling situation, a good salesperson will relate to the buyer in a way which makes the buyer comfortable. Of course, this comfort zone is different for each situation, but must include respect, caring, and an information exchange, all at the level the buyer requires in order to feel comfortable enough to say "yes."

Recently, someone asked me if I enter into a conversation with a (potential) customer with the idea of "getting a fix" on who she is so that I can sell to her in a way that will make her buy. That interpretation is a gross misunderstanding of what I believe, and it would make my approach manipulative. While I use the information a person gives me about herself to get into rapport, I then go on to set up a relationship. As this is not a relationship in the true sense of the word, I call it a "we space," *an environment structured by the needs, values, and beliefs that the two people interacting agree to, having different parameters than those in which either operates individually.* Any two people can create a "we space" within a short period of time, so long as the *values* of both people—what I call the *criterial* rapport—are respected. The earlier you can set up this shared environment, the sooner you can discover if a person has a need which your service or product can support.

My approach is based upon respect, not manipulation: respect that the person I am speaking with knows—or will know—what is best for her, what she wants and needs. Sometimes the information needed to fully examine all the issues involved may not be readily accessible. Sometimes a customer's map does not include all the information needed to give clear choices. This is another reason to be genuinely curious and nonjudgmental. When you ask nonjudgmental, curiosity-based questions, a customer willingly lets you know her beliefs and thoughts around your product and expertise. You can actually help organize her experience around the subject by asking the appropriate questions, ensuring that her answers will lead her to explore her problem areas for herself. When you stay separate from the content, and remain in control of the structure, you can hear if this person has needs which are not being addressed, and you might ask further questions which will address them. You may also lead her to new ways to approach her existing problems, and she just might look to you to help supply the answers.

It gets tricky here. We deal with our product or service in numerous types of applications, probably more varied than our prospect's. We can often see applications or services which they cannot see, which would enhance their environment or lives. But we have a very limited understanding of our prospect's circumstances. Our job, then, is to create an environment where we can explore both of our knowledge bases. Before we are given the right to discuss our product or service and how it relates to the prospect, however, we must attain trust and rapport. We must discuss the particulars of her environment—budgetary constraints, personnel and politics, time frames, priorities, and long-range plans--in order to get a complete picture of the issues. Prospects are happy to discuss their constraints and problems, even after four minutes on the phone, if a "we space" is first created. And from this place of relationship, a prospect trusts that she has the same goal we do: to ensure that she gets what she needs.

Maps Revisited

Let's explore in more detail how "maps" affect relating to clients with respect.

To maintain relationships with customers, I have to accept their view of reality, their "map," as the truth and work from there. If I don't, I'm out of criterial rapport, as our basic beliefs and premises are not harmonious. A student recently suggested that by getting into another's map, she would be giving up her personality and therefore be dishonest. Our personalities are part of our identities, part of who we are. Matching maps is done on a behavioral level. Let me give you an example. A friend of mine recently told me that the man she was dating told her he liked her to style hair off of her face. For her, that was a simple change in behavior. But when he requested that she let her luxurious brown hair—in actuality prematurely gray—grow out into its natural color, she balked. She did not see herself as an old woman (which, in her belief system, was equated with gray hair).

We needn't conform to another person's map, just have a good understanding of it. When I hear a potential customer tell me she believes that nobody needs to learn telephone skills, for example, I am fighting a losing battle if I try to convince her otherwise, as she will certainly go into defense mode. But if I can step back and accept what is being said with just an "Ah, that's interesting," I voice acceptance, if not agreement, and we remain in rapport.

This is one of the major differences between selling and building a buying environment. The old, traditional sales approach is about convincing someone to buy your product or service, whether or not she has interest or believes she has a need for it. In a buying environment, however, the buyer's beliefs, needs, and values are what's important. Our job becomes helping people help themselves.

I once tried to convince a prospective customer that what he perceived as adequate coverage in his service department was, in fact, a wrong perception. We got into a battle of wills, and I tried, in every way I knew how, to say the right words which would make him realize the error of his ways. Needless to say, he fiercely defended an indefensible position, and I lost a potential customer. Here's the conversation:

Client: We're doing really well. The work is getting out, everyone is happy, and we are just about on budget.
SDM: Yes, but you are misappropriating your staff. If you

had my people in there doing the programming, you could free up your staff to get on with the exciting parts of their jobs and the department could be expanding instead of stagnating. And if we did the work for you, you'd be so productive in the other areas that you'd be well under budget. [Note: I am telling my client that he's got it wrong and that I know better than he does.]

Client: People understand that every job has it's exciting parts and its boring parts. What's important is that we remain a team with no outside interference. We're now discussing if we want to get the additional work done after hours. The staff only has to work double shifts a few times a year and they don't mind it. And we'd save the money you'd charge us. I really can't see any reason to hire in from the outside.

SDM: Mainly because you'd be more efficient. [Note: I'm saying that he's inefficient.]

Client: Are you saying we're not efficient? We've got the highest productivity in the company. I should give you some other names of less efficient people to sell your services to. We're really doing just fine, thank you.

Does this sound familiar? It's obvious what happens when I try to be right, to try to sell something which, if purchased, makes the client admit that he's not doing his job properly. Through my need to convince and to sell from my own map, I make him feel defensive. We are out of rapport, and a "we space" cannot be established.

The next time a similar situation occurred and someone told me he had it all covered, I agreed with him, helping him to defend his belief. After he heard agreement from me, he backed down. (During the conversation, I also assisted him in organizing his experience while supporting his map and building a buying environment.)

Client: We're really okay in that area. Plenty of work gets out, there's little turn-over, and I stay pretty much within budget.
SDM: It sounds as if you are doing wonderfully. I hear that

you really don't need any outside help.

Client: I wouldn't say that. We could always use help.

SDM: If all of my customers were as pleased as you are about their in-house systems, I wouldn't have any work. I'm impressed with what you are doing.

Client: Thanks, but it's really not totally true. To be honest, in our area, we're a bit behind and could probably use a little help. Could you tell me about your project management services, or would you recommend something else for the kind of help I need?

SDM: Let's gather some information here before you decide you need help. What is it precisely that you feel is the problem area? And if you had all your wishes, how would it be different?

In this conversation, I worked from acceptance to acceptance, helping the client discover his needs in his own time and in his own way. I opened the opportunity for him to buy what he needed.

In his book *On Becoming a Person,* Carl Rodgers asks the following questions in terms of understanding another person's belief systems (Note: words in parentheses have been slightly modified by the author as to gender):

Can I let myself enter into the world of the (customer's) feeling and personal meanings and see the world as (s/he) does?

Can I step into (his/her) (map) so completely that I lose the need to evaluate or judge it?

Can I enter into this person's reality so sensitively that I can move about in it freely without trampling on meanings which are precious to (him/her)?

Can I sense this (map) so accurately that I can catch not only the meanings of this experience which are obvious to (him/her), but those meanings which are only implicit, which (s/he) sees only dimly or as confusion?

Can I extend this understanding without limit?

Unless we can let go of our own prejudices and accept that another person has a different way of viewing the same situation, and that her way is equally valid, we cannot fully relate to someone whose stated experience is different than ours. The more we are convinced that our way is right, that we know what's best, and attempt to convince someone that she is wrong, the more the other person defends her right to maintain her belief—and the sooner we lose a client's business, or a staff person's loyalty. By operating this way, **we can only sell to people who share the same belief system and values we have and we thereby limit our buying audience.**

This is where most business people get in trouble and may find themselves saying, "I don't like this person," "This guy doesn't know what he's talking about," or "I can't be bothered with her." In this mode, we have the attitude that if a client doesn't buy when it's clear (to us) that she should, we either reject her, or, if intent on getting the business, learn better and more effective ways to convince her. We call it "negotiating skills" or "the gentle art of persuasion" or "overcoming objections."

But the other person is as sure of herself as we are and resents us knowing better. The trick is to form a "we space" with her, facilitate discovery of her areas of need that are within your area of expertise, and respect her choices.

Skill Set 2

Relationship

1. Think about your personal beliefs around creating and maintaining a relationship on the phone. Under what conditions would you think it possible? Impossible? Are you willing to examine these beliefs?
2. List what is comfortable about speaking with friends on the phone. List what is uncomfortable about speaking with strangers. Note any differences in the comfort level between the two. In order to alleviate discomfort, the differences must be minimized. (The skills necessary to achieve this will be addressed in the chapters ahead.)
3. What would you need to re-evaluate in order to take on the premise that it's possible to use the phone for relationship-building?
4. Remember conversations you've had with people where there has been rapport, and conversations where there hasn't been. What are the differences between the two?
5. Selling and buying come from relationship, not approach. Think about the differences in your own career between sales which have come out of an established relationship and those based on convincing. Have you been able to maintain long-term relationships with these people?
6. What are the differences in your behavior, voice, language patterns, and body language you used during your phone conversations, when you had a "we space" with a customer, and when you just tried to sell something?

Rapport

Chapter

3

People will buy what they need. With that belief in mind, sales calls are easy: help the person find out what he needs, create an environment of agreement so that he feels comfortable with you, and if he needs what you've got and is in a position to buy it, he'll buy. Simple.

As a salesperson, though, I was trained to convince. That generally meant I answered objections, told well-woven tales about what I sold, and found ways to get and keep attention—all to let the prospective client know that my product, service, or information was the right choice, and that if he did not buy it from me, he was making a mistake. That approach was based on the assumption that the buyer made bad choices in his purchasing decisions prior to our meeting; either he paid too much, got a product of inferior quality, or was inadequately serviced. I thought that it was my job to convince someone that I was better, and for this I used my own selling patterns, rather than discovering the prospect's buying patterns.

I used any opportunity to get in a plug for my product, and in doing so, violated one of the most fundamental rules in communication: I was not operating from the customer's map. Using that approach, I had success only with the people who would have chosen to use my product anyway, who were similar to me—in needs, voice, personality, beliefs, and approach--and who were already in agreement. Sales were based on finding enough people who operated out of *my* map. But unless the initial rapport was strong enough for us to continue speaking after the sale was completed, the sale would not be repeated. The relationship was random. How could I reach all the people who needed to buy my product and who did not respond to me or my approach?

Once I realized that I could change the random nature of my interactions, I could facilitate any buying situation, with any buyer or any product, in person or on the phone. I did this by:

- entering into the map of the buyer
- taking responsibility to create the environment which would give the client the freedom to discover his own needs with my assistance.

I began to appreciate that whoever owns the problem owns the solution. I made it my job as salesperson to help the client discover his own solution. You can do the same.

Breaking Down The Behaviors
In Comfortable Situations

While training myself to establish a comfortable environment for cold calls, I noted that I would never treat friends the way I was taught to treat my customers. I had a "we space" with my friends. We were just as comfortable speaking on the phone as we were in person.

A successful conversation entails people being in sync, and the behaviors take place on an unconscious level. When we have difficulties in an interaction, it's usually because the differences between us outweigh the similarities. Since you are learning choices to control the times your conversation *doesn't* work, let's take a careful look at your *successful* behaviors so you can learn to replicate them.

While breaking down feelings of comfort when speaking with friends (you might have done this in Skill Set 2), notice similarities in your vocabularies as well as your voices (tone, tempo, volume, and pitch). Friends speak quite similarly and rarely notice the similarities. In fact, we are only cognizant of any discomfort when there are differences. People unconsciously assume others will be the same as they are and notice differences because differences take them out of rapport.

Rapport
The trick, then, is to learn how to be in sync with strangers in order to feel comfortable. And **rapport** means being similar enough not to notice the differences.

In a face-to-face meeting which is going well, we unconsciously sit, talk, and use body language similar to the other person's. We are even more comfortable when our values, beliefs, and goals are similar.

Matching And Mismatching
In order to be in rapport with another person you must share comfort on three levels: **physical** (voice and language patterns); **mental** (shared interests); and **emotional** (beliefs, values, and goals). When you and your customer are similar on any or all of these levels, you are said to be **matched.** It is more comfortable to be around others who are in agreement with us and therefore hold an unstated mutual respect and acceptance of us.

Recently, I had a conversation with a man who clearly did not want to be speaking with me, and, try as I might to match our voices and beliefs, he was not participating in the conversation happily. I had a sudden brainstorm and mentioned that I was glad I lived in Taos this year instead of his hometown of Denver. We had 130 inches of snow! He laughed delightedly, and the ice was broken. He obviously had a greater need to be matched around his hobby of skiing than he did around work.

Once matched with your customer, you can make shifts in ideas, conversation content, or actions *and have your conversation partner make the shifts with you,* so long as the shifts maintain the specified outcome and are done through rapport. In other words, when you start from a place of mutuality and then veer into a different mind set in order to introduce an idea which may be uncomfortable or foreign, you can assist your partner in comfortably examining a different map, so long as you remain in rapport in voice, language, and goals. This is a very powerful concept and must be used sparingly and appropriately. In fact, I only use it with established customers, never on cold calls, as introducing an opposing reality can be jarring and you need an established foundation to fall back on in case it doesn't work.

Other people—a distinct minority—prefer to be mismatched. This becomes apparent very early in a conversation. These people look for the difference, to find the place to disagree. Nothing you can say will be left alone without something found to be wrong. It is difficult, but not impossible to deal with this type of prospect.

A face-to-face example of this occurred during a consulting project I was conducting. The CEO sent a memo to all the Board members, asking them to meet with me for three hours. One of the members canceled our appointment several times. When the appointment finally took place, I entered the office and he said in a blustery voice, "Look. I do not agree with what you are doing and I have no wish to waste my time with you. I'll give you fifteen minutes." From his body language, I could see he was doing the opposite of everything I was doing, and I knew he would continue to do so. So I responded in kind, and sat down in the farthest chair, even though he was still standing. My voice was tough and pompous. My body was away from his. Since he liked to be different, he sat in a chair close to me, and softened his voice. I kept us hopping for almost four hours, always changing voices and positions, as well as topics. I never allowed him more than a few moments to settle in. This kept him comfortable. This kept me in charge. He did not know I was in charge, and that in fact, we were *matched* as I mirrored his behavioral criteria.

In Chapter 10, Helpful Hints, we will cover matching and mismatching when handling problem calls.

Voice And Words
As discussed earlier, to achieve rapport on the telephone, you must sound similar to the person you are speaking with—at least until the rapport and relationship grows over time. This means

consciously making behavioral choices to sound similar during cold calls, new client calls, and incoming and return calls with strangers who have questions and complaints.

Initially, get the *volume, tempo,* and *timbre* of their voice tone. Then get the *cadence.* You may feel awkward and uncomfortable at first, but with practice it will become second nature and rather fun. It's important to mimic the initial "hello" and continue with a similar voice until the content of the conversation flows between you and your customer instead of being piloted by you alone.

Remember the statistics: seven percent of communication is words and thirty-eight percent is voice. That means, the *way* the words are spoken is five times more important than what the words are. If we take these percentages and extend them for phone use and delete the body language percentage (fifty-five percent), that puts eighty-two percent of the onus on the voice; only eighteen percent on the words! I continue to be amazed at the number of companies which spend months training their people on content—months of up-front learning in all aspects of insurance, years of technical training to sell computers. But I know of very few companies that teach their people how to listen, how to ask questions and how to establish rapport. With all the technical expertise in the world, if salespeople can't connect, a sale can't be made.

People forget specific words, but they won't forget the feelings the words leave behind. In fact, it is generally not crucial to have all the specifics of your product or service at your disposal during the initial call, though obviously specifics are vital when it comes time to take or fill an order. When I consult with people in a one-to-one session, I often do cold calls with people using their list. I almost never know enough about their product or industry to say more than a few words about it, but it never seems to come up. My job at that point in the calling process is to call a prospect to establish rapport and a "we space," gather information about his environment and perceived needs, and set up a trusting environment. The words and content I use relate only to facilitation, not product.

Choosing voice volume is crucial. If nothing else, make

certain your voice is at the same level of softness or loudness as the customer's. If your voice is much louder, you will sound over-powering. If softer, you sound weak.

Sometimes I shift my volume as a way of mismatching, to get attention or to convey either power or submissiveness. When I was running my company, I called a man who was in a position far below mine and used a very soft, gentle voice to create an environment for him to empower himself in whatever way he needed to in order to feel equal. As a company president speaking with a line manager, I was the one in control from a status standpoint, but since I wanted him to buy something from me, he, in fact, was in control. So I spoke softly, and even hesitantly, to let him steer the conversation. I never forget that in each conversation, the buyer has the power.

Cadence and tempo are also important. Have you ever tried to hang on to a conversation in which the other person spoke much louder or softer, or faster or slower than you? Begin each conversation by matching voice as close as possible. Then, keep it up until you have achieved a similarity of values.

Criterial Rapport

A more sophisticated way to be in rapport is through *criteria*. In fact, once a similarity of values is established, physical/voice matching is not so critical. Criterial rapport is very powerful, and every successful relationship—between clients or between friends--must include a shared system of beliefs and values.

When we first meet people, we may be drawn to them for various reasons: the way they look, their personality, or what we've heard about them. But if we cannot abide by what they believe in or stand for—what's important to them—we prefer not to further the relationship. In business relationships, we often cannot afford the luxury of choosing to discontinue a relation-ship because of someone's differing beliefs.

People's values are very individual and often eccentric. Politics, religion, the environment, and health issues are all areas where people make individual choices. When a relationship you are building demands criterial rapport—which automatically happens when you work with your client to assist him in solving his stated problem--it is necessary to find a way to accept, promote, and enhance the client's understanding of his business needs. There may be instances when you choose not to continue dealing with this person, when doing so would cause you to disrespect yourself. But there is a foolproof way to circumvent this issue: structure the "we space" around common work issues.

Skill Set 3

Rapport

1. Notice those people, in both personal and professional relationships, with whom you are in rapport and those with whom you are out of rapport. What is the difference between the two sets of people?
2. What do you need to know about an individual in order to want to be in rapport with him? Are there people you work with daily with whom you are continually out of rapport? What specifically makes it difficult for you to be with these people? What would they have to do or think differently for you to accept them? Consider behaviors *you* would have to adopt in order to accept them.
3. Examine your client base. Are there people you have a difficult time with? Consider any criterial similarities you could gravitate toward to help your relationship with them.
4. During your calls, get into a voice match immediately through your volume, tone, tempo, pitch, and cadence. Although this is a conscious process for you, the person on the other end won't notice anything other than a feeling of sameness. (It is not necessary to continue with the match throughout the call, just until criterial rapport is reached.)
5. You will recognize criterial rapport when the conversation takes on an easy flow and you are unaware, or unconscious, of trying to do anything different than be who you are. Note in several conversations how long it takes you to get into criterial rapport. Are there time differences between conversations with people you know and cold calls?

6. Maintain a "we space" by working from agreement and continually summing up the information you've gathered.
7. Internally, continually monitor your client's comfort level. Has his tempo changed? The volume? Are the two of you regularly taking turns speaking? Is he getting interested enough in you to ask you questions? Are you matched criterially?

Respect

Chapter

4

If you try to convince a potential customer that you know what's best for her, you are being disrespectful. It might work once, but if you are planning to retain this client over time, respecting her capacity to solve her own problems works better.

Sometimes a salesperson rationalizes her approach by saying that her clients don't know what they want, and she believes she knows better than her clients about what they need. I don't believe that to be true. However, there do exist occasions when there is a discrepancy between the client's present and the future situation, and the client cannot discern the issues clearly because she is lost in the present situation or busy defending it. When that discrepancy exists, by definition there is a problem, and it will have to addressed at some point by your prospect. Through rapport and questioning, you might be able to help her in examining the problem, and your product may (or may not) be the appropriate solution.

A friend recently came to me with a problem. She was selling radio advertising and was having a bad month. She explained how stupid her potential clients were because they were not buying into a rate special for the month. She could not believe they were not interested. When I asked her how she was approaching people, she told me she had been patiently explaining the benefits of the deal. I then asked her to describe the problems each of the prospects was having in her business and she became silent. "I never asked," she said.

Whoever Owns The Problem
Owns The Solution

When we remain disassociated (able to hear a problem as if we had no attachment to it), we can ask questions which get the client thinking along new paths and examining new perspectives. Whoever owns the problem owns the solution. It becomes a trap when we attempt to solve problems which are not ours, as we end up being held accountable for any problems which occur as part of the solution, **even if they are beyond our control.**

Working From A Curiosity Base

The easiest way I know to get into another's map is to ask questions based on genuine curiosity, rather than just gathering information to use in a programmed selling or closing technique. I ask questions about a client's job and environment: people, job descriptions, politics, problems and the process by which they are solved, lines of authority, and so on. The more I learn, the more curious I become, the more the other person talks, and the more trust is developed between us.

Remember that most of what is heard during a conversation is generally forgotten, and we remember only the general outline and feel of the conversation. However, you can greatly increase your retention if you don't do all the talking. Let the client do most of the talking, while you help organize her thoughts and experience. Your call then consists of framing appropriate questions which will lead to discoveries of what that person needs *for herself!* From that point, you will work at viewing the situation *from the client's perspective rather than your own.* (This will be discussed more fully in Chapter 6, Questioning Techniques.)

I recently spoke with a student of mine who called out of quiet desperation. She had had a good first call with a prospect which led to her sending him a video of the team-building program she was offering. When she made her follow-up call, she was given a cheery "hello" and was told that her tape gave the man evidence that his team was in fact doing very well, and that while he now realized he didn't need her services. He'd passed the video on to a colleague with a note that she'd call him. She was pleased by the results, but when she told her boss, he was angry.

"You had him on the phone! Why didn't you *convince* him he needed the program!"

I believe the saleswoman was successful and that not every client needs what I have to sell. If I have made enough of an impression on someone after a cold call to get a high-level referral, I am satisfied. For me, that's a win-win situation.

Choice Through Perceptual Shifting

There are times when I am convinced my clients are wrong. My inclination is to set them straight or stop working with them. However, if my outcome is to maintain rapport, and the relationship I'm building, I have to remove myself from the battle of right versus wrong, maintain my outcomes and goals, and not worry about or respond to the bits which are content. My criterion remains that *I don't want to be right, but to be in relationship.* Because this behavioral choice is so vital to a respectful relationship, let's discuss how to disassociate yourself in order to work from a curiosity base and not take things personally.

Association Versus Disassociation

To have flexibility and clear behavioral choices in any interaction, you have to learn how to *disassociate.* This removes you from the content of the conversation and give you the perspective you may otherwise lose when you're caught up in your own personal beliefs and value judgements. An objective observer's vantage point allows room for a nonjudgmental information-gathering and rapport-building interactions, ones which create or maintain long-term business relationships and include trust and respect.

In the past, when I became *associated* into a situation— directly involved in the content—I could not see my own behavior patterns. I behaved in a random manner that worked or didn't—with no choices for when it didn't. These situations did not benefit me or my client, and I often ended up with an irreparable problem.

As I learned to understand and appreciate the differences between being associated and disassociated, I found that I could choose to travel between being locked inside my own map, beliefs, and values (*associated* into what I call Self) and being an Observer of my behaviors and therefore *disassociated*. I could remain in relationship with people whose maps were different from mine without feeling that my beliefs were being stepped on. I became infinitely flexible around behavioral choices—a necessary skill when I was taking responsibility for the interaction.

I learned to recognize the behavioral signals which let me know that it was time to disassociate. I used two sets of triggers: physiological and auditory. When I noticed myself sitting forward, hunched over with my head down, and feeling tension in my body, I was generally associated into Self. The opposite was true for a disassociated state: I was more open and sat back with my head up, with little tension. The auditory signs were easy to notice: I found myself getting annoyed with the person to whom I was speaking and trying to convince her to see things my way.

When clearheaded, I was able to understand that when an otherwise nice, competent person acted in ways I found easy to judge, I was missing information. Therefore, as soon as I heard annoyed or blameful conversations inside my head (directed at the other person), noticed my mind racing to find ways to convince the other person she was wrong and I was right, or heard myself speaking aggressively, manipulatively, or angrily, I checked my body posture for signs of being associated. If both body and mind were giving me the same signals, I knew I was associated into the issues. I used these triggers to recognize when it was time to pull away and "take myself to the movies."

I taught myself to see a blank movie screen in a large movie theater. I then put characters who looked like me and my phone partner on the screen, and put myself in the audience, wearing a director's cap. From the vantage point of the Observer, I could watch the interaction. The people on the screen were so caught up in their own maps that they had few behavioral choices. They had no distance with which to get perspective on the structure of their interaction. The disassociated person watching in the audience (me) had the distance and perspective to see the whole picture and create new choices and behaviors for the actors on the screen. I learned to give that familiar woman on the screen the flexibility to back down, ask more questions to get an understanding of the client's map, and allow space for mutual agreement and the potential of really being available to provide a service.

Here's an example of using disassociation to handle a difficult situation.

While working in his office one day, a British CEO received a call from a very irate woman calling from Rome. I could hear the shouting through the receiver from across the room. I watched while the man in front of me attempted to counter everything this woman was throwing out, point by point. He couldn't keep up.

"But Francesca, I *sent* that . . . "

"But you said you got that three days . . . "

"Didn't you remember . . . "

She kept screaming, and he kept attempting to intercede with explanations. The conversation was obviously getting away from him. I went over to his desk and wrote him a note, whispering to him to repeat the words before him. He looked up at me and made a mocking face. "Say it!" I encouraged. He rolled his eyes, shrugged his shoulders, and said, "Francesca, I hear you're frustrated."

Silence from Rome. A big sigh. "Well, I just needed to let off steam. Don't worry. I'll take care of it." She then hung up.

The CEO was surprised. "How did you do that?" he asked me. "How did that work?"

I explained that when we are lost in the content of what someone is saying to us, we are associated into the conversation and behave according to our own maps and needs. We don't have the distance to see behavioral choices and are therefore unable to move the conversation to a place of resolution. When we can disassociate, we get the broader picture and then deal with what the person is *really* saying—what I call the underlying message or the meta-message, or reason she is speaking with you. In this example, if the woman really wanted the man to deal with each point she was making, she would have left ample opportunity for him to do so. Instead, she spoke loudly, jumbled the points on top of each other, did not wait for each topic to be addressed before going on to the next, and disregarded the CEO's comments. Since it was impossible to deal with the issues being shouted, what was her meta-message? Clearly, the meta-message she put forth was that she needed to make her anger and frustration felt, and the words she chose were but a vehicle to get to the feelings. By remaining associated, it was impossible for the CEO to notice the emerging patterns. We will look at this important concept in Chapter 5, How Conversations Work.

Creating The Environment

Once you learn the difference between being associated and disassociated, you can become more aware of your responsibility to make certain that the client is given the climate to explore her choices. It is possible to set up an *environment* to help your client get new clues or new ways to approach her problem. Once you enter a "we space" with your client or prospect, you can disassociate and ask questions which surround the issue, giving her room to start thinking of alternative solutions—all from her own map, of course.

Let me give you an example of how this is done. During a luncheon, the head of a major airline's department of end-user services mentioned to me that she had six programmers. Knowing she also had 2,000 end-users, alarms went off in my head: it was an impossible task for only six computer people to adequately support the programming needs of 2,000 people. However, it was not my job to tell this highly-paid, top executive that she got it wrong. Instead, I noticed the alarm bells and used them to disassociate and help her find her own answers.

"Could you explain to me how that works, with so many users and so few programmers?" I asked out of curiosity, as my disassociated self had no answers and made no judgements. I worked from the assumption that this executive knew something I didn't.

"I wish you hadn't asked me that," she replied.

I changed the subject, knowing the question had registered, that I had started her toward solving her problem, and knowing that if she needed an external solution, she would use my company's services. My client and I had built up a relationship over time which gave her the understanding that I cared about her—not just about getting her business.

The next morning I called the woman.

"Hi. I got an idea. Do you believe you need to know how the programmers and users interrelate?"

"Yes. I think I've been avoiding looking at the problem."

"How about if you get one of the company consultants to do a survey of the user community, and find out what's going on— in terms of duplication, or work not getting completed, or people not doing their assigned tasks just to get the computer reports completed."

She thanked me, telling me she was thinking along the same lines. We hung up, and I knew she would find the answer herself.

Two weeks later, she called. She was unable to get the use of a company consultant and wanted to hire one from me. It was a $150,000 job. And I didn't sell. My customer bought.

This story is interesting on many levels. It is a fine example of how you can act as a buying facilitator. On another level, it's an example of disassociation. I knew what she needed from the initial conversation, but also knew it would have been inappropriate and unacceptable to give advice. I trusted that she was intelligent enough to find the right solution. It was my job to set up the environment within which she could explore her choices and needs and discover her own solution.

Skill Set 4

Respect

1. Take an inventory of people closest to you. How similar are they to you in beliefs, behaviors, likes and dislikes? What patterns have you established with them around your differences? Do you sit down and discuss? Argue? Agree to disagree? Ignore the issues? Compromise? Under what conditions do you do each?

2. Remember specific interactions you have had with two or three people with whom you have ultimately chosen not to be in a relationship. How were they different from you in beliefs, values, behaviors, likes and dislikes, or other specific ways? How did you deal with your differences? Did you talk about them, or didn't you bother? What made you decide not to further the relationship?

3. What were the differences between the above two exercises? How do you choose friends? What are your beliefs about differences of opinion, being right or wrong? Are you willing to look at bridging the gap between being wrong or right in order to maintain and create relationships with your customers?

4. Notice what happens internally when you feel you are right and someone else is wrong. What do you feel? What are your behavior patterns? Notice any resistance to giving up your need to be right in order to maintain or create a relationship.

5. In your mind's eye, picture yourself having dinner with someone you care for. Do you see two people, and are therefore disassociated from the picture? Or do you see just the other person, and are associated into the pic-

ture? Switch positions. What is the difference? How does each make you feel? What would you need to know, believe, or practice in order to be able to switch between being associated and disassociated at will?

6. Make a picture of a blank double-movie screen in your mind's eye. On the left-hand screen, make a picture of a successful phone conversation with a client. On the right, make a picture of an unsuccessful call with a prospect. Notice the differences in the pictures separate from their content. Check the pictures for differences and similarities in color, sound, and clarity. Look at your body language in both pictures. Do you notice physiological feedback? Internal dialogue? A tension in a specific area? Differences in your voice? If you can discern differences in the pictures of the calls, you can duplicate the successful call and make a choice to disassociate by replicating the physiology of the successful call.

7. When you are able to make a conscious decision to learn a new skill around being right or wrong, and decide to learn to disassociate, practice the "movie theater" technique. Then make up your own disassociating technique. Decide which is most comfortable for you and use it regularly. Make sure to build an internal trigger (a feeling or word reminder) that signals when it is time to disassociate.

Section Two

The Hows

How Conversations Work

Chapter

5

The phone is a wonderful tool. Information can be gathered from both sides, people can get to know each other, and decisions can be made, all while carrying on with your normal day and not even leaving your desk. However, to enjoy the freedom of using the phone to create and maintain relationships that will sustain the level of business you desire, you must have the flexibility to speak comfortably with anyone, in any type of business situation.

Rapport

As with most conversations, phone calls follow a simple rule. First one person speaks, then the other: "A"—"B"—"A". Both people generally do not speak at once. Because this etiquette is understood by anyone using the phone, the salesperson can use the rules to encourage, create, and enhance the rapport between buyer and seller. The salesperson must learn how to use silences, turns, questions, voice modulation and volume, interjections, and timing to encourage the buyer to speak.

Moving From Agreement To Agreement

When you gain rapport with the other person, you are both matched. Moving from agreement to agreement is infinitely easier than from disagreement to agreement. It becomes a win-win situation for everyone: the prospective client gets to take a few moments out of the day to summarize the present or problem situation and to either take further action or consolidate his position. You get a chance to assist him in organizing his experience and looking at future needs (as well as to increase your chances of either doing business or getting a referral).

In the past, I often found myself invested in saying the right thing to get a specific response. To do this, I had to listen closely to each word in order to counter the objections or get the sales pitch in at the right time. When I learned how to operate out of curiosity rather than manipulation, and understood that my only job as a buying facilitator was to create a comfortable, supportive environment which could help a prospect discover for himself any unmet needs, I could then sit back and listen to the conversation on a structural and behavioral level.

Organizing The Experience Of The Buyer

For years, we, as buyers, have been conditioned to defend ourselves against salespeople in order to give ourselves the space we need to decide for ourselves. Imagine if we, as salespeople, help create that space. In this way, we *organize the person's experience*.

The buyer can often use our help in structuring his thinking process around possible needs or potential problem areas, as he sometimes gets bogged down in his present situation. Since adults generally prefer to believe they make adequate decisions for themselves, it is important for us to let our buyers remain in control of the content of the call. We do this through our questions and by responding to customers and prospects in a way which keeps them on the topics we wish them to think about, thereby giving us control of the call's context. (See Chapter 6, Questioning Techniques.)

This is not so easy as it sounds, especially when we feel we are experts in our field and the potential buyer doesn't know as much as we do. We may feel certain we have the answers and they don't. We must remember that we only have the answers for ourselves, operating out of our filters, our map, and a perfect world. In our reality we have no budgets to organize, or politics to play, or deadlines to meet, or cutbacks, or hiring freezes, or corporate training schedules—all the things our clients face everyday.

It is also important to keep your buyer talking as much as possible. Again, this not only aids his thinking process, but also gives you information to understand his criteria and goals and evaluate how he thinks, speaks, and acts on his ideas.

I cannot emphasize enough that the purpose of each call is to find out enough about the prospective buyer to know if there is a fit between you. The easiest approach is to remember that each person has a turn to speak. Be sure to either ask a question, sum up, or find a way to agree when it's your turn to speak. Then, the rule is that it's the other person's turn. For example:

Prospective client: I really don't need any more insurance. I'm completely covered.
Sales person: That's great. If all of my prospective customers were as well covered as you, I wouldn't be in business.

The difficult part for most sales people trained to convince is to *end the sentence there.* You face potential silence when you give up an opportunity to sell and instead act as a buying facilitator to create a "we space" where your prospective client may—or may not—choose to buy. But *now it's the other person's turn to speak!* And speak they do. I have found that when people no longer need to defend an indefensible position, they give up defending and take a look at what their needs might really be. There may be a more realistic way to evaluate a situation than the approach they've been using, but they might not see it until your call gives them the opportunity to look at it with a fresh perspective. Sometimes they back down, with something like "Well, maybe I should take a look at my coverage again," or "Maybe it's time to review the situation."

I have found that sometimes the people who have the most to defend are the people who end up buying the most. This became apparent to me when I noticed how active my dead file was. So long as you stay in agreement—no matter how difficult it may be, even if it's just to say "I hear that"—you maintain the "we space," stay in rapport and matched criterially, and recognize the other person's map as different from but equal to your own.

Another scenario which can happen is when the person understands that he has been given the opportunity to take a moment to look at his present situation and realizes that, in fact, there are no needs. By assisting your clients in discovering positive aspects of the work environment, you will be appreciated for the respect you offer. This scenario, of course, enhances your relationship and widens the "we space." You are also given an opportunity to ask for a referral. And since the prospective client finds you non-threatening and easy to converse with—with seemingly similar beliefs and values—referrals come easily. You will also be remembered when a future situation finds the client in need of your product or service.

Let's break down the components of conversations in terms of what's necessary for continued behavioral choice. We've covered some of these topics before, but we'll now examine them in light of how to maintain control of the context or structure of any given call. We'll examine how conversations work in specific contexts (cold calls, for example) in the Applications section.

Breaking Down The Call

Once you realize that your job is about facilitation, not convincing, the phone will become a terrific time-saver. Since you have no way of knowing in advance what the specific content of any conversation will be, you do not have to be totally conversant on any particular product line, although product knowledge is ultimately vital. (In the past, I spent much time gaining vast amounts of product knowledge which was wasted if I couldn't get into rapport or get a conversation started.) By preparing for the relationship rather than the task, you have a better chance of bringing in more business.

But you do have to prepare for each call in a new way. Clear your mind, disassociate, and be ready to receive this other person, listen to his voice in order to match it, get into rapport as soon as possible, and know which questions to ask in order to engineer and direct the conversation's structure.

Use the following steps for each call you place. We will go through the steps again more thoroughly in Chapter 8, Listening, but these will get you started. Try to examine my approach with an open and curious mind, as it may run counter to approaches you have been taught to use. Use the parts which you can comfortably adapt into your current style. Use Skill Set 5 to pinpoint the differences between your successful and unsuccessful behaviors, and take the skills I've offered to navigate the difference. Flexibility is the issue here. Richard Bandler, co-founder of NLP, states that when there are behaviors you cannot generate, there are responses you cannot elicit. The "Law of Requisite Variety" holds true here: the person with the most power in any communication is the person with the greatest flexibility of responses.

One more thing to remember: approach each call with the SAME outcome: *to create an environment of rapport* in which the person on the other end of the phone gets the support he requires to discover his needs. As the buying facilitator, remaining curious about this person and remembering that you have nothing to sell unless he has something to buy is the most difficult aspect of this approach. When I pick up the phone with some idea of what I'm going to say (unless I'm calling for a specific reason, say, to break an appointment or reconfirm an order), I'm on the road to a bad call.

Clear Your Mind

Clear your mind completely before dialing. If you begin with preconceived ideas about what you will say, you will miss what the other person is telling you. You can only attend to one person talking at a time, and if you are talking to yourself, you cannot hear the other person.

Say A Matched Hello

Listen closely to the voice of the person who answers. **Say "hello" by matching the voice identically.** This is the only way to get into immediate rapport. *Make sure you match the volume and tempo.*

I prefer to be the person placing the call, since the person on the other end must say "hello" first. This gives me the opportunity to make mimic the "hello"—it may be cheerful, quick, annoyed, deep, soft, loud, forceful, gentle. With my first word, I communicate to the person on the other end that he and I are similar. Many times in a busy day, I have answered my own phone for the seemingly hundredth time and brusquely and annoyingly shouted my greeting, only to be met with a sweet, gentle or cloying voice that I knew immediately I did not wish to cope with. If the person's tone is just as brusque, I know I will only have to give my attention for a few moments—*but I will take the call.* If the person doesn't say something like "I hear you are busy, can I make an appointment to speak to you some other time?" I will quickly make myself unavailable again.

The topic of voice and matching tempo is an important one and will be expanded upon in Chapter 8, Listening, with specific how-to examples.

Draw A Mental Picture

If you feel more comfortable on the phone with someone if you know what he looks like, **begin to make a mental picture of the person** after you match your phone partner's "hello." It doesn't matter if the picture is accurate. Initially, just guess. With practice, it will become accurate.

Introduce Yourself

Introduce yourself by name only, and ask in a style, volume, and tempo which approximate the prospect's initial voice, if he has time to talk. If not, ask for an appointment to call at a prearranged time. I usually throw in a bit of casualness here if at all possible in order to sound like a real person and to get into rapport more quickly.

Develop The "We Space"

If asked, tell the person in a word or two what you do ("I sell insurance," or "I am a trainer"). Then **turn the conversation back to the prospect** by asking if they currently use the product or service which you are promoting ("Do you have insurance?" or "Does your company run seminars?").

Here is where most salespeople go wrong. They begin *selling* their product at the first opportunity to speak, before they have agreement or rapport. If you get sucked into "selling" your product here, understand that you have inadequate rapport and inadequate information on which to base a sales pitch. You will be operating solely out of your selling patterns, not as a buying facilitator. But once the prospective buyer begins speaking, you have begun to establish a "we space."

Let him know in some way you think the two of you have things you might talk about and you'd like to tell him what you do—but *first* you'd like to hear about his needs or solutions to problems your product solves (i.e., "Can you tell me what kind of insurance coverage you have?" or "Can you tell me something about your in-house programs?"). You might offer here that you'll go first, if he wants you to, by saying, "I can tell you what we have to offer, but if you want to tell me how you are covered first, we can see whether or not I have anything which can help you."

If the client speaks first, remain disassociated and ask questions—lots of them—about his current job or problem. With each question, be sure to listen to his answers and allow him to complete his thoughts before asking another question. While he is speaking, make sure you get a good understanding of the context this person operates out of by asking yourself these questions: is he or she the decision-maker? What is this person's comfort zone around admitting and noticing problem areas or needs? *Why is the person taking his time to speak to you?* You may ask your prospect questions such as: is there a difference between his present situation and a desired state? Does this person ever hire outside consultants? Is there a budget? Who has been taking care of his needs in your area?

If you speak first, give a very brief, generalized run-down on your product or service ("We sell specialized types of insurance dependent upon a person's specific needs . . . " or "Our courses are tailored . . . " or "The equipment we sell can be geared toward specific environments and problems"). End your statement with, "But I'm not sure if you need to buy this from me now." After all, you don't, and you are at a disadvantage since you don't know what parts of what you offer fit with this person's possible needs.

Maintain Rapport

Notice shifts in the volume and tempo of this person's voice. Shift your voice accordingly and, from a disassociated position, try to discover the reasons behind the shift. Questions you might ask yourself to stay disassociated are: is the conversation getting uncomfortable? Is there a time problem? Have I said something from my own map? Am I out of rapport?

If you are out of rapport, get back into rapport by first matching voice volume and tempo. Then begin summing up what you understand to be true of the client's perspective so far. Occasionally ask if what you understand is correct ("Can we take a moment here and backtrack? What I hear you saying is . . . . Did I get this right?"). This will get him back into his own frame of reference and speaking about himself. It will also give you the opportunity to see where discrepancies are.

Address Only Specific Needs

Remember to only address that part of your service capacity which will be potentially interesting to the customer, even though you may believe that your product could address additional needs.

If you have been the one speaking, ask the prospect if what you do interests him enough to tell you more about his needs.

If the customer has been speaking, notice when he begins to ask questions or gives you the opportunity to speak. Usually, when the other person talks for a while and has answered your questions, he will be pleased to give you your turn at speaking and answering.

Note that by the time you have a two-way conversation, and the prospective buyer is answering your questions, you have successfully created a "we space" and are responsible for maintaining it.

Follow Up

Once it is clear *to both of you* that you have common areas of interest, and you have spoken for a few minutes about the aspects of your product or service which interest your phone partner, **begin to disengage from the conversation by asking the client where you should go from there.** Trust the relationship. He will tell you precisely what is needed (for example, written information or a call on a certain date). If he suggests that you wait until information is received and will call you back, ask if he'd feel comfortable if you called him if you don't get a call back in, say, a month. We will review this strategy in Chapter 9, What To Say When It's Time to Talk.

Get A Referral

If the prospect believes you have no reason to work together, ask if he knows anyone who might be interested in your services. If your rapport has held up throughout the conversation, there is at least a ninety percent chance that he will give you a referral. I'd still be curious about why this person spoke with you for so long. I'd have a suspicion that while the current situation was fine, he was not addressing a possible future problem and is storing your information for future reference.

Make Future Plans

Unless the call has been a failure all around, **always end the call with some type of future plan:** to speak by a certain date, to touch base when a referral has been contacted, or to send something by mail. I send some material, my card, and a little note with a "Thanks for the referral." In this way, you maintain your relationship. Business may result some time in the future, either directly or indirectly.

Remember, there are some calls that are doomed, no matter what method you use. When this happens, THROW THE NUMBER AWAY.

Skill Set 5

How conversations work

1. Take notes of a conversation you initiate with a friend. Note the patterns of both speakers, and if, when, and how they change:

> **Voice:** Volume, tempo, cadence, tone, and pitch
> **Turns:** Who speaks first, most, most often? When and how do interruptions occur?
> **Outcome:** What did you want from the call? Did you get it? Why? Why not?
> **Internal Dialogue:** Are you talking to yourself during any part of the call? All of it? Are there any consequences when you do? List them.
> **Frame:** At what point in the conversation do you tell the person why you've called? Do you launch into a monologue? How does the conversation begin? How does it change direction or topic through content changes, questions, or voice shifts?
> **Shifts:** What kind of changes take place during the call in content, voice, tone, and time frames (present or future)?
> **Future Pace:** How do you end the call? Which of you makes the request or commitment to have future contact?
> **Picture:** Do you maintain a mental picture of what your friend looks like? Does it shift or change or disappear during the course of the call?

> Do this exercise during several calls with friends and take notes during each call.

2. Repeat the above exercise with business calls . How do they differ from calls with friends? How are they the same? Are there differences between calls with clients you know and cold calls? Clients you have met and those you have not met yet? It is important to be clear on the differences—in voice, content, comfort level, pictures, internal dialogue, turns, and outcomes—between speaking with people you know and people you don't.

3. Begin to use the suggestions recommended in this chapter. Use the ones most similar to what you already do comfortably. Begin to add the new ones you are most comfortable with.

4. Itemize the aspects of the call-handling method in this chapter which you find uncomfortable. Choose one aspect a day to incorporate into your conversations. Practice this aspect all day.

5. Practice, practice, practice.

6. Note the aspects you have great difficulty adjusting to. Are you able to take on any new skills when speaking with friends but not with your business calls? What's the difference? Are you unable to adopt these methods during any call? If you had to make a guess, how would you change your behavior to successfully adopt these methods? Are you willing to make these changes? Do you believe it is worth it? Do you believe it is possible? How would you get help making a change? Remember, if your belief system tells you that something is impossible to achieve, it is.

Questioning Techniques

Helping A Client Discover Her Needs

Chapter

6

We don't have answers for our customers, although we'd like to believe our product or service will address their needs. But we certainly can ask the questions that will help them find their own answers. *The more we can create an environment in which our clients can discover their own answers, the more trust will exist in the relationship.* In fact, our questioning skills should enable our customers to continue their train of thought and further develop their thinking.

I currently spend about seventy-five percent of each conversation asking questions and listening to the answers. Questions **encourage** people to be concrete and specific, thus helping them **organize** their experience, **discover** their own problems and/or solutions, and **enhance** the client/supplier relationship. Questions also **clarify** and **direct** the conversation, giving you the basic control of the call. After all, you are the one responsible for creating what you want in the call. And finally, questions allow you to **understand** another person's map which is different from your own. This helps create the "we space" from which the customer can explore new options for problem-solving. Because your questions assist your client in organizing her experience and uncovering her problem areas, a buying environment is established.

Using Self, Observer, and Other
To Aid The Questioning Process

Managers often have difficulty clarifying problems and solutions due to environment, colleagues, budget issues, time problems, political considerations, and so on. In other words, they have difficulty disassociating in order to discover how to accomplish what they believe needs fixing. In fact, just because they believe something needs to get done doesn't mean they are able to accomplish it with the means the company makes available. But I've found that I can sometimes help them disassociate and possibly explore new avenues by asking the questions that get them to look at their problems from new angles.

The hardest part is remaining curious and unbiased when choosing which questions to ask and pinpointing what information needs to be elicited. In the role of "salesperson," you probably have perceived your job to be based on the product or service you are selling, rather than, as a buying facilitator, supporting people in getting their needs met—regardless of whether or not your product is involved. Given that your questioning processes have historically been based on gleaning enough information to illuminate a need you can directly sell into, the method I put forth may go against much of what you have been taught. Yet we use this method freely in our personal lives.

Imagine being out for the day and calling home to ask your spouse if she needs anything. She says "yes." "Great," you reply. "I'll be home in an hour," and hang up. Let's say you walk in with a large box of styrofoam peanuts. *"What's that?"* asks your spouse. "Well, you said you needed something, so I decided to bring you this." You would never think of behaving this way at home, and yet salespeople do this all the time. They decide what their clients need based on their own map and never collect the data which will help their prospects get the information for themselves.

One of the internal systems which either aids or prevents us from being able to get into someone's map is the amount of flexibility we have. *Unless I can move away from my own ideas of right and wrong and enter an internal state of choice, curiosity, and*

respect for differences, my positive relations with others will be based
solely on the areas where our maps interconnect. I am most successful
at remaining curious and unbiased when I develop the ability to
move between three positions: my own beliefs (**Self; associated**);
standing back to notice where and how another differs from me
(**Observer; disassociated**); and being willing to step into the
other person's shoes (**Other**). In any job involving relationships,
this skill means the difference between being good at what you
do and being great. It's the ability to have infinite flexibility of
behavioral choice. It means being able to sustain rapport with
anyone.

Shifting Positions

Traveling between these three positions seems like a cumbersome task, although we do it intuitively in almost all activities. In
this chapter, we will break down the position shifts into gross and
separate stages, so you can learn to use them consciously.

In our most successful conversations, we regularly shift
positions but do it so quickly that we aren't aware of it. In fact,
when performing any behavior, skill, or hobby at the level of
excellence, we are moving between the three. If we do not travel
between these positions, our achievement is less than what we'd
expect, as when we are in a learning situation and haven't yet
learned the parameters of our subject well enough to move away
from being associated with it. We are, therefore, still in Self.

For example, the difference between my paintings and those
of a master are that a master switches between the subject
(Other), the canvas (Observer), the idea (Self), the paint (the
medium) and his eye (Observer). When I paint, I get stuck in one
of the places—usually the idea and Self—and cannot move on.
Another example is skiing. When I am thinking about where my
arms are (too often facing uphill), I stand a greater chance of
falling than if I operate as whole, with my body (Self), the snow
(Other), the skis (the medium) and the picture I make of how I'm
doing it all (Observer) coming together. On the telephone, I am
often able to operate with excellence, since I'm able to perform
these shifts regularly and consciously. There is no difference
between my thoughts and internal dialogue (Observer), the

client (Other), the questions I ask (Self), and the receiver (the medium).

A video expert taking one of my phone skills courses was having difficulty taking the Observer position. I asked him to think about the role of the camera when he was on a job. He realized he made an unconscious choice on setting the scene, made decisions about its content, and then comfortably travelled between his eye (Self), the camera (medium), the subject (Other), his vision (Observer), the blocked-out shot (Other), or his arm adjustment (Self). He had just never realized he had been moving between the three positions. Once he was conscious of his behavior, he no longer had difficulty understanding how to do it with the phone.

You must make the shifts conscious before traveling between the positions becomes unconscious, and it can be uncomfortable.

Because using these three positions (Self, Observer, and Other) with conscious choice is so important, let me explain each of them further, how they work together, and how they can be used to enhance the sales process.

Self

I find that when I listen for content alone I remain in **Self**. That's the place where my personality resides, so I am actually listening through my own personal filters. When I speak to people in my private life, it's easy to just be myself, since there is a good chance their maps are similar to mine. But when I want to connect with a client or prospect, the more flexibility I have in accepting another's map, the more I can connect in a way which will be comfortable for both of us.

By remaining solely in Self, with little flexibility to expand your range of acceptance and understanding, you will only connect with the same percentage of people time after time. When you cannot be flexible around sharing maps, the chances of a sale are slim to none when speaking with someone whose behaviors, attitudes, or beliefs are different from your own. In programmed selling, people have always said that using the phone for sales is a numbers game: the number of people who need your product *and* will acknowledge it to you *and* feel immediately comfortable with you is but a percentage of the population *and therefore random*. If you believe that your products and services can serve many more people than that, you will have more success if you make the **behavioral choice** to enter into another's map and **alter your behavior in ways which will leave the acknowledged need the only variable in the sales process.**

The more time you spend in Self when confronted with people who are different from yourself, the more likely you are to judge, compare, attempt to solve, and perceive the interaction through your own set of beliefs. This pits **you** against **them.** It is here you might think you understand precisely where and how the customer has gone wrong and needs to do it all differently, (most likely using your service).

Observer

In the **Observer** place, I am honestly curious about the other person *without a hidden assumption that she needs my product and that I can find a way to get her to use it just by asking the appropriate questions.* From this place, I ask myself questions which need to be answered, such as why this person is speaking to me, what seems to be her main concern, if there seems to be a presenting problem, or what information am I missing to further assist the customer.

When you are able to step back into the Observer and disassociate, you have the choices which allow you to know what questions need to be asked, what information must be elicited, and what sequence of questions you should use to help the customer get the information she needs in a non-threatening way. I do this by keeping a running internal dialogue about what appears to me to be the underlying message—the meta-message. What is this person *really* saying to me? (A simple example of this is when a prospect continually forgets to return your call. This is a clear unspoken message of disinterest.)

Putting Self And Observer Together

Here's an example of a conversation in which I assisted the prospect in uncovering his problem space by stepping out into Observer to understand his meta-messages.

Client: We really don't need any more copiers now. [A time factor contingency is obvious here.]

SDM: Does that mean you will be needing them later? [The question clarifies the time factor.]

Client: Probably.

SDM: How will you know when it's time to take another look at the situation? [Again, I continue with questioning in the area my customer chooses to highlight. I do not understand fully what **now** or **later** means to him, nor what I need to know about **time** according to his map.]

Client: When we hire more people.

SDM: So when you take on more staff, you will know to buy more equipment. [I'm summing up what he's said here. I personally still don't have a clear understanding of his time frame.]

Client: It won't be right away. I guess I won't really be ready until I hear complaints that there are too many people using the equipment. Then I'll know it's time to make a change. [It is still not clear to me that he knows exactly when he will know or what he needs to hear— number of complaints, from how many people, and so on—to make a decision.]

SDM: It sounds like you've gone through this before, and you're waiting until the staff complaints work for you. [Again, I'm trying to fill out the complete picture. I want to know the exact pattern in order to understand how I can assist the process. Also, if we can break down the pattern thoroughly, he may realize there are more options available other than repeating the pattern.]

Client: I have. Actually, I think I waited too long last time. By the time I went looking for additional equipment I had some problems to deal with. [Here is the problem space which the customer is realizing himself. My response can assist him in finding his solution.]

SDM: I wonder if there's another way to do that which would work better for you. [I'm opening up a space for the client to examine his own option.]

Client: I might begin looking at the equipment first and be ready to place the order when I hear the first signs of grumbling. That should save me some problems. [He's open to the possibility of doing something different to get different results.]

SDM: Would you be willing to take a look at my equipment to fill those needs? [I need to get agreement that he would indeed be interested in working with me. Until now, he's talked about time and equipment, with no specific reference to his supplier.]

Client: Sure.

SDM: What would be the most comfortable for you? Would you like to call me when you are ready for a demo, or have me send information about the machines, or send you an invitation to our next customer evening where all the copiers are demonstrated? [I always believe the customer knows how to proceed to get what she wants. It's my job as supplier to make the options available.]

As you can see, by traveling between **Self** and **Observer**, I set up the structure of the questioning process through my curiosity. I asked questions based on what seemed to me to be missing information. If there was information missing, the customer discovered it with my help. I did not presuppose to have the answers.

Other

The **Other** position gives me the opportunity to remain in rapport with my customer and to perceive things just the way she would in order to get quality information. Unless you are truly able to get close to the full perspective of your customer, your thinking and judgment will be one-sided.

From Other, you can know how the comfort level of the conversation is progressing by going to the other side of the receiver and into your customer's shoes. I actually imagine myself looking like my client does, sitting at a desk, talking to Sharon Drew Morgen on the phone. And I feel what it would be like to consider the emerging issues. From this envisioned seat,

I monitor the following:

- *relationship issues*—Do we have a "we space"?
- *rapport*—Are we similar and working toward the same goals?
- *language patterns*—Are we using the same sentence structure and vocabulary?
- *voice anomalies*—Are there differences in voice tempo, volume, and tone?
- *content shifts*—Do we continue speaking about the same topic or does it shift?

Obviously, I must be disassociated to be able to get to the other side of the receiver, and this helps in recognizing how my behaviors are affecting the call.

Why do I do this? To get a clear understanding of the interaction from my phone partner's perspective when she is engaged in describing possible trouble spots in her environment. When do I do it? When there seems to be a break in the rapport; when the prospect asks me a question and I want to get a clearer idea of what type of a response will assist her; when the prospect asks me a question and I want to understand if I am missing any pieces of information which I need in order to answer appropriately; and when I ask the client where we go from there and I want to maintain our rapport at the conversation's close.

Consciously entering the **Other** state is not something we are accustomed to. We tend to either sympathize and empathize intuitively, or we operate most comfortably out of our own maps. Having the choice to get into the mind set of the Other will give you additional information and increased rapport. It requires taking a non-judgmental look at your own behaviors and making adjustments accordingly.

Putting It All Together

When I have optimal flexibility—the ability to speak comfortably and create and maintain rapport *with every potential customer*—I move between Self, Observer, and Other consecutively and concurrently. Here's what I do. In the **Self** position, I get curious. By using **Observer** I know to flip through my mind and compare the background information I have on the person and subject matter with what the person is saying. I actually sort for the differences between what I then believe to be "true" and what my phone partner believes. I notice holes in my understanding, get curious as to the differences, and ask content-based questions to fill in the gaps. If there are any information gaps which emerge, the customer will notice and begin examining what may be a problem. When I feel objections or shifts in the conversation I go to **Other** and do a rapport-check to become aware of any issues.

By alternating between Self, Observer, and Other, I will know which questions to ask and what information needs to be elicited. Here's how it happens.

1. The Self starts to compare my beliefs about what is possible or needed against what I'm hearing from my phone partner.
2. Through internal dialogue, the Observer keeps me curious and nonjudgmental through disassociation.
3. By getting into my client's shoes, I maintain a running checklist on the Other, noting values, beliefs and comfort needs while paying attention to shifts in voice, sentence structure, and breathing.

By using the three positions simultaneously and consecutively, I can continually monitor the quality of information I am receiving and decide which questions to ask to facilitate the next piece of the discovery puzzle for the customer.

Skill Set 6a

Traveling between Self, Observer, and Other

1. Name a skill/hobby which you perform with excellence.
2. Note which functions you perform from the Self position. What parts of your behavior do you perform automatically?
3. Note which functions you perform from the Observer position. What questions do you ask yourself to check your progress?
4. Note which functions you perform from the Other position. How do you know when you have to make a shift in behavior?
5. Notice shifting between the three. How and when do you do it? In which position is it easiest to operate with conscious choice? Which is hardest?
6. What would make it possible for you to be able to shift between the three positions at will?
7. Remember a time you were having an argument on the phone. Make a mental picture of this event. Record the voice quality (volume, tempo, tone, pitch) and your body posture from this picture in your notebook. Try to remember the gist of the conversation and what you may have been thinking of. Note the amount of freedom you had in making different behavioral choices during the course of the argument. Note any comparisons or judgments. This is the Self position.
8. Remember a time when a stranger approached you to get directions. Note your ability to listen with curiosity and without judgment. Note any internal dialogue you had. Did you make any judgments about the person asking for directions? Note your voice and body pos-

ture. Note your freedom to make behavioral choices for yourself. This is the Observer position.

9. Remember a time you were comforting a friend by just listening and supporting. Were you aware of their feelings? Were you aware of their comfort with you? Note your voice and body posture. Note your freedom to make behavioral choices for yourself. This is the Other position.

10. In the above three scenes, compare the differences in your physiology, beliefs, behavior, judgment, voice quality, and body posture. Note these differences (between Self, Observer, and Other) on paper and place the sheet on the wall near your desk.

11. Think about the differences in your behaviors and physiology in the three positions. Begin to notice when you are using Self, Observer, or Other in different situations during the day.

12. Imagine a specific difficult business situation, either in person or on the phone. In your mind's eye, practice using the body posture, voice, behaviors you use in Self, Observer, and Other, and begin to adopt the behaviors and physiology of each position. Note any difficulties or triumphs. Note which ones are easy or hard. Which positions do you use randomly? Most frequently? What do you need to learn to give yourself more behavioral choices?

13. Begin adopting these behaviors and stances consciously during daily interactions. Start with easy, comfortable interactions. Before you progress to more difficult ones, make sure some of the shifting between positions is starting to come naturally. It might take days or weeks of practice. Be aware of the difference it makes in your ability to make decisions, to remain in rapport, to solve problems, to understand another person's map, and to empathize.

Now we can begin to look at how we go about asking questions from a place of curiosity to facilitate the client's discovery of her needs. I will be using Self, Observer, and Other to help explain the steps.

Assisting Clients In Recognizing Their Problems

It is imperative that you ask assumption-free questions in order to not prejudice your beliefs about the needs of your prospect. When asking assumption-free questions, you can:

- help a client organize her experience
- get an understanding of the client's map and how it differs from your own

When you hear a problem that the client does not perceive to be a problem, it's vital you acknowledge the problem from the viewpoint of Other. Clients often defend an indefensible position by stating that everything is fine, or the problem is being taken care of whether or not it is. When this occurs, increase the rapport by agreeing that the problem seems to be well in hand. As discussed earlier, when there is nothing to defend, your client has permission to back down and ask for help. If enough information, trust, and rapport have passed between you and your customer, she might choose to examine the problem space, search her environment for resources, and possibly buy a solution from you if none readily exists.

I recently had a conversation with a man who was deciding on whether or not to take one of my programs. It was an archetypal conversation in that he found all his own answers to his problems with just a bit of facilitation from me. Since he was expecting my call through a referral, he was able to comfortably make small talk for the first thirty seconds. I began framing the conversation the first chance I got:

SDM: I hear you have some interest in my Phone Skills program. [I am setting the parameters in a non-aggressive way.]

Client: I do. Would you tell me something about it?

SDM: I'd love to. But first tell me something about you and what you use the phone for. [I really do not know what he wants to hear me speak about or the information I need to know about him and his environment which would keep us in rapport. Therefore, I do not take this as a speaking opportunity. Most salespeople would launch right in to selling what they want this person to buy, and see the opening as a selling opportunity.]

Client: Sure. I work for an actuarial firm as the salesperson. I'm the only person in the company not licensed in some form of accounting out of a hundred people in this office. I use the phone daily to set up my real work— getting appointments and doing the face-to-face.

SDM: It sounds like you are doing fine. What would you need my course for? [It was difficult not to point out the error of his ways immediately—that he was underusing the phone and wasting a lot of time. I wanted him to recognize the problems for himself. Also, there might be something about his environment that I didn't know and that would explain why he didn't use the phone to qualify potential clients.]

Client: Well, I find I have a lot of discomfort on the phone, and I sometimes don't know how to get past my introduction.

SDM: What's your introduction like?

Client: I give people my name, and introduce my company.

SDM: Give me an example.

Client: "Hello. My name is Steve Johnson, and I'm with Grow International. I'd like to tell you a bit about my company."

SDM: I get it. That would make me uncomfortable too, both as a seller and a buyer. [I'm taking a risk here, as I might be going too fast for him. But our rapport level is extremely high, and he seems to be seeking answers.]

Client: What would you do? [The conversation is now turned around: he's taking responsibility for the questioning.]

SDM: I never introduce my company, and barely introduce myself. I figure if the person I'm speaking with doesn't know me, she or he won't be interested in who I am. I get them speaking right away by just giving my name and asking if they have phone skills courses.

Client: That's really interesting. What about my discomfort? Would that change my discomfort level?

SDM: Are you uncomfortable speaking with me? It feels real good from this end. [I'm making him realize that he is perfectly capable of being comfortable and creating comfort.]

Client: You're easy to get comfortable with.

SDM: What's the difference? When I called you, I didn't know you and somehow we both managed to remain comfortable. You got into rapport with me instantly. Was it all me? [I want him to realize there is no difference between me—a stranger—and a prospective customer.]

Client: I didn't even realize it. Maybe I didn't feel pressured by needing to get an appointment with you.

SDM: I'm curious about something, if I could digress for just a moment. Of all the people you get appointments with, how many actually buy? [I am taking another risk that a negative answer on his part would break our established rapport.]

Client: Not many.

SDM: So you keep calling to make appointments and going out to visit people who will probably not give you business? [Here I am summing up what he told me—just mirroring the content.]

Client: I don't know how else to do it. [Honest guy.]

SDM: Do you recall the beginning of our conversation when I asked the questions? I was qualifying you— gathering enough information to stay in rapport with you through your voice and what was important to you. How long did it take? [Here I am letting him see that I teach what I do—and that he was comfortably involved in the qualifying process without realizing it.]

Client: Seconds.

SDM: Are you interested in taking my course? [This questions is a set-up: I'm giving him the opportunity to see how what I do works.]

Client: I think so.

SDM: And I haven't told you a thing about it yet. All I've done is asked you questions about you, your job, and your work style and let you find out the problems you are experiencing for yourself. You decided you needed more information to be more successful, and that working with me felt good. [Here I am assisting this man in disassociating.]

Client: You're right. I didn't even realize what you were doing, and I'm already ready to buy something I need from you without even knowing anything about the course. That's amazing. Could you tell me about the course now?

By demonstrating the questioning process, I assisted this man in uncovering new potentials for phone usage.

Organizing Experience Through Questions

How can questions be used to assist someone in recognizing her needs—some of which might not be apparent at first glance? How can we organize the buyer's experience through questions?

When I started my career, I used questions as a set up: Do you use my product and are you happy with it? What did it cost you? Who supplied you? How does it perform over time? How are you being serviced? I used the phone to try to accurately position by product and make it clear that she'd make a mistake by paying too much or by not buying it from me.

In this way, I was able to get business only from people who were in agreement with my evaluation and didn't mind my telling them that they'd blown it. The other people who would respond to this style of questioning were those I had accidently gotten into rapport with and who felt relaxed enough to tell me what they needed. It was all random. It worked when it worked, and I had no control over the times it didn't.

What I was doing, in fact, was entering the customer's problem space by attempting to offer her my own solution. My entering at this level was task oriented and ignored the problem-solving process the customer needed to go through alone.

As buying facilitators, our listening and questioning skills should enable a customer to continue her own train of thought as a result of our conversation. A customer will have her own answers once she can utilize all her internal computations, as well as organize and access all her relevant historical information. Questions will also unearth important, quality information which your customer might already know but hasn't considered. I believe individuals often have much of the information needed to make a decision. We just don't always have it organized in a way in which it makes immediate sense to us.

In his book *Tell Me a Story*, Roger C. Schank says, ". . . the process of communication itself can alter what is being communicated (pg. 234)." He also writes, "No intelligent system is likely to function effectively if it cannot find what it knows when it needs to know it . . . . the vocabulary must be employed in a description of themes, goals, plans, results, and lessons (pg. 112)." And ". . . people know . . . implicitly what questions not to bother asking themselves because they know they cannot easily find the answer (pg. 70)."

By trusting that the person you are speaking with is intelligent, and by asking her the questions that will help facilitate her own solutions by accessing stored information, we can garner a client's support in assisting the sale.

The Questioning Process: An Overview

Before I went to Wall Street, I was a social worker. I believed my job was to instruct, advise, support, and counsel, and I took this belief with me when I began work at Merrill Lynch. There was a big difference between the two jobs, however. While I felt comfortable supporting my patients, I didn't know enough about the financial world to feel confident when speaking with clients. I would ask and ask and ask questions to get customers to the point where they'd tell me what they needed rather than have me advise them—and opened more new accounts in six months than anyone in their first year in the history of that branch—even though I told the prospects I was new and might lose money for them.

What Information To Base Questions On

The questioning process I use to assist in the relationship-building and discovery acts like a funnel for information, going from the general to the specific, from the present to the desired situation, bringing me and my client closer to a problem area.

A side benefit of this process is the ability to retain control of the parameters of the conversation: since the objective is to facilitate solving a problem for which the solution might involve your product, take responsibility for keeping the conversation structured around the area your product supports. It's not your direct intent to assist in problem-solving in a conversation around buying office furniture if your product or expertise is in another area.

Other considerations are deciding what information is important enough to warrant questions, and how and when to interject.

How and when to interject is the easy part. As long as you remain in rapport—voice first and then criteria—you can use any appropriate opportunity (when the prospect completes a thought) to ask a question or make a summation. The specifics of how this is done will be discussed in the next three chapters.

Deciding what information warrants questions is more difficult. As a salesperson, my questions were manipulative. As a buying facilitator, though, my questions are different: what information does my prospect or client require in order to assist her in discovering what she needs to buy? The formulation of your questions should be structured to illuminate any problem areas which might exist in your client's environment. Your questions, therefore, should more clearly define your client's present situation and give you both a common understanding of the environment in which you might be working. When I do this, I find it easy to stay curious. I create a mental technique to help me "see" what the client is telling me. I actually take the information I receive, put it into puzzle-shaped pieces, and fit the pieces into a space which looks like a blank movie screen in my mind's eye. Wherever I "see" a piece missing, I ask another question. My goal is to get a clear picture of my client's environment (politics, staffing, problems, budgets, timing, and so on). Therefore, my questions come out of a real curiosity and don't seem manipulative to my prospect.

The Step-By-Step Process

In order to get a more in-depth understanding of how questions can facilitate the "buy," let's take a look at the stages involved in the questioning process.

The Inviting Questions

The type of question most useful for initiating a conversation and gathering introductory information are *Inviting questions*, used to invite the client into conversation. They can be informal if you already know the client ("How have you been?") or formal ("Is this a comfortable time for you to have a conversation with me?"). In both instances, when the other person answers your questions, she enters the conversation in relationship. In fact, the questions invite collaboration. Note, however, not to ask someone you have never spoken with before, "How are you?" This question implies an existing friendship or some intimacy. Since you do not know the person yet, it is invasive and requires that she speaks to you before you are in rapport.

At the onset of a conversation with a prospective client, inviting questions should be geared toward rapport-building and gathering preliminary, sometimes logistical, information. Depending on the situation, the questions I most frequently ask are:

- Are you the correct person I need to be speaking with?
- Do you have time to speak with me?
- Would you like to speak first, or should I?
- Would you mind telling me about your environment?

My Inviting questions to an existing customer are different and more personal in nature, and I will probably mention something personal about myself as well. I am immediately involving myself and this other person in a "we space" and my reason for calling is to enhance and continue an already-established rapport. Here are some examples of questions I use in this instance:

- Is this a good time for us to speak?
- Have you been bearing up under all the strain?
- How is the new program working?
- Do you find that the product or service is making a difference?
- Have you discovered any more information you need from me?
- Could you tell me about what has happened since we spoke last?

Whether speaking to a prospect on a cold call or a long-time client, this initial stage in the phone call gives you time to listen for content around the client's present environment—company culture and politics, and language patterns, as well as time, cost, and quality needs, values, and manpower—and the opportunity to understand if there are areas of problem and defense. It is during this time that you also pick up her voice pattern to get into voice rapport.

Facilitating Questions

Once the conversation is underway and it is clear by the match in voices and the amount of information shared that the customer and I are in rapport, I get actively involved in the process which will lead to the discovery of a problem—even in the early minutes of a first call. The call proceeds from initial and somewhat superficial information-gathering to defining the client's environment. *Remember, in order for you and your client to move toward a solution, your client must know exactly what is happening in her present environment.* Most clients are so involved in the detail of their environment and its patterns that it is difficult for them to step back to notice things aren't necessarily working to achieve their outcomes. In fact, people often are so beleaguered with day-to-day drama, they lose sight of their outcomes.

Facilitating questions help the client or prospect organize her thoughts to inspect the present situation and long-term goals, possibly using my product. Once this person is directed toward the specifics of how the pieces of her environment fit together to produce a goal, the magnitude of a possible problem state emerges. And the responses give *me* a clearer understanding of the operating environment so I know what questions to ask next.

The Step-By-Step Process is demonstrated in the following example (which continues through the rest of this segment).

I recently asked a prospective client, a harried company president, if he felt comfortable always feeling so pushed. I used facilitating questions—along with the ever-present *summary questions* which we will get to later in this chapter—to help him take a serious look at how his current decisions affected his company.

> *SDM:* You've been telling me how busy you are each time we speak. What are you getting out of working this hard? [This question must be asked with real curiosity, not judgement.]
> *Client*: Well, it's all on my shoulders and I don't have a choice. There is no one else to do this particular work. [He's getting to do it all himself. He's not given himself another choice.]
> *SDM:* How long have you been working at this level of frenzy? [I'm giving him the opportunity to look more closely at his behavior.]
> *Client:* Quite some time now. Let's see. I guess it's four or five months.
> *SDM:* Are you enjoying it? [Again, curiosity here.]
> *Client:* Not really. At first I thought it was seasonal, but then it didn't let up.
> *SDM:* It sounds like you are committed to continuing to do it all yourself. [Summary question]
> *Client:* Not really, but I promised myself I would never have more than eight people working for me, so I can't

hire anyone else to help.

SDM: Interesting. So I hear you saying that your business is growing but you cannot hire help because then you'd have over eight people in the company. [Summary question]

Client: Correct.

SDM: What is important to you about having a company with only eight people? [I don't know if he understands the full extent of consequences around his decision-making.]

Client: If there were more people, the company would be too big, and I wouldn't be on top of everything and the business would get ragged.

SDM: So now, with eight people, you know what's going on and can stay on top of everything you want to stay on top of, is that right? [Summary question]

Client: Theoretically. But I'm so damned busy that I can only keep track by coming in on weekends. And I still am not able to keep it all under control.

SDM: What do you see as the company's future? Do you plan on limiting business so you can keep the staff small? [There are many information gaps here that are causing me confusion. I've not met many people who have this kind of criterion around limiting the size of a small and apparently growing company.]

Client: I guess it's more important to me to continue supporting my customers, as I am one of the only people in my field. I really love what I am doing and being involved the way I am. I guess committing myself to serving my clients is more important to me than keeping the number eight inviolate. So if I am already growing, my real problem is not finding more time for myself, but whether I can raise the number of staff in a way which would maintain control of it. Thanks.

My outcome in this part of the conversation was to facilitate this man's thinking process, to let him take a good look at his present situation in relation to his continuing problem and future outcomes. He was so wrapped up in fighting fires he didn't even realize there was a difference between where he was and where he had previously stated he wanted to go. My questioning helped him organize his experience and find his own problem space.

Examples of Facilitating questions I use most frequently and the areas they address are:

- What is important to you about . . .? (cause)
- How is that important? (cause)
- If you could do it or have it the way you want, how would it be? (effect/result)
- What does this get you or do for you? (effect/result)
- What's getting in the way of your creating your solution now? (uncovering obstacles)
- What stops you? (uncovering obstacles)
- What happens when . . .? (exploring obstacles)
- What would happen if you do or don't? (exploring obstacles)
- What do you need in order to . . .? (evidence)
- How will you know when . . .? (evidence)
- What would you need in order to . . .? (resources)

Customers have told me that when being asked these above questions they are initially slightly uncomfortable, as the information being elicited is often not readily available to them consciously. But only rarely do I encounter a situation in which a prospect will not answer my questions. They flow easily and comfortably within the "we space" I create, offering trust in my genuine curiosity and desire to assist them. It is then possible for them to comfortably explore their problem in a new way.

If I do not complete the first phase of information-gathering and rapport-building adequately, the person I am speaking with will feel pushed. When I hear or feel annoyance, I know I am going too quickly, and I back down by asking a light information-gathering question or by requesting that something be explained again for me.

Specifying Questions

Once the customer begins to delineate his experience, specific facts, issues, and problem areas need to be reexamined or defined. A different type of question works best here. I call them *specifying questions,* and they usually begin with the word **What**. They are about defining, differentiating, and enumerating.

- What do you mean by . . .?
- What would you need to . . .?
- What stops you or helps you?
- What's the difference for you between X and Y?
- What would that look, sound, or feel like?
- What would you accomplish out of doing it that way?
- What obstacles do you see or feel would come up?
- Is what you have in place giving you what you want?

These questions bring you and your client to the beginning of the search for a solution. Facilitating questions promote the exploration of the current environment and future outcomes, while Specifying questions help the customer begin to understand the task of problem-solving and how specifically it can or cannot be accomplished, given the available resources.

To continue with my conversation with the harried company president, let's note how the conversation changes when the specifying questions are introduced.

SDM: You're welcome. What would you need to know in order to raise the number of staff and keep control? [Although I am remaining within the framework the man has chosen, I am pushing the structure a bit to have him look at his own issues around any behavioral change he would need to accept in order to bring change to his company.]

Client: I guess I'd have to have a good support structure in place for hiring, training, and supervision.

SDM: What would that accomplish? [He's not sure because these are just the issues he didn't want to deal with in the first place. I want him to fully understand the possibilities for personal comfort as well as success. His fears are more about control than service.]

Client: That would free me of the direct, daily responsibility for the new people and would keep the company running smoothly while we were growing. Also, I'd only have to know what was going on with the managing staff rather than each person individually.

SDM: So you'd add more people but not have to be personally responsible on a management or time basis. [Summary statement]. What would the new company structure look like? [I'm having him look at the future to see the differences between his present situation and his future one. He'll also begin to recognize the resource needs he'll have to face.]

Client: Well, I guess I'd have to add a management layer. That would also mean bigger offices at some point.

SDM: Are you aware of any obstacles in doing that? [Here's an opportunity for him to back down, to acknowledge personal needs or discomforts. He may have already overcome those, in which case he will name task-related obstacles as opposed to feelings.]

Client: Yeah. Money. Time.

The business problems are beginning to emerge now through the process of clearly defining the details of getting where he wants to be. The next set of questions examine the dissipation of the obstacles.

Organizing Questions

I now closely and specifically question the resources it would take to solve the problem. Once it becomes obvious to the client that there are questions without answers, my questions become very specific: *How* do you plan to accomplish this? *Where* will you get the resources to complete that?

Organizing questions bring even greater specificity to the tasks involved in solving the problem. These questions are about time and action:

- What would need to be in place for that to happen?
- What would you do first?
- Do you anticipate a problem getting the resources you need?
- What would help you solve that piece of the puzzle right now?
- What would be your first step in creating that for yourself?
- How would you go about solving that problem?

By now, there is a pattern emerging: my client and I have gotten into rapport with each other, entered into the information-gathering process, facilitated an exploration of his environment, and contributed to his finding answers by asking questions about tasks and step-by-step solutions to solve the problem. *It is here that customers will notice an absence of available in-house or personal resources which would solve their problem.* In my experience, many people do not generally go through the entire process of specifically defining how to get from here to there, and when they do, they are amazed to learn they need help doing it.

Let's continue with our conversation using *Organizing questions.*

SDM: How would you go about solving the problems of time and money which you'd need in order to increase your staff and change the management structure? [It's important for this man to examine how he plans to get from his present situation to his desired one.]

Client: I don't have the answer to that now.

SDM: Try guessing. [People always have the answer on a guess, so long as they don't have to admit they are committing themselves to anything.]

Client: Well, I'd have to put together a new budget to see how the hiring of new staff would affect the bottom line. I'd have to layer in the new people over the course of, say, a year. I don't even know yet how many new people I'd need. I'd have to sit down with a pencil and paper and write job descriptions, figure out pay packages, decide which departments would grow, which ones grow first.

I guess I'd be reorganizing the whole company.
SDM: So what would you do first? [Step-by-step.]
Client: Take a look at where I want to be in a year and two years. Then sit down with the management structure to see exactly what position would need to be filled first.
SDM: What you are saying is you want to examine all the parts that need to be looked at and changed over the course of time, right? [Summary question] Can you make any changes which would help your situation now? [He is really going way out there. I must attempt to bring him back to the present, as it's easier to move in small increments.]
Client: Hmm. I guess I could start delegating some of the work to my assistant. She's been asking to take on more responsibility and I've wanted to do it all myself. That would take some of the pressure off. She's good. But I still have to decide the best place to find good people.

Several problem areas are emerging for this man, problems he didn't know he had when he started the conversation. The questioning process brought him to specifics about where he is, where he wants to be, what he needs to do to get there, and what problems need to be solved in the process. In this case, there was no need for the client to buy any services from me. He gave me two referrals, however, one of which led to a closed sale.

Supplementary Questions

During the questioning process, it is important to make sure you understand exactly what your phone partner is telling you. Since the words the other person uses may have a different meaning than the meaning you would ascribe to them, you have to make certain there is a mutual understanding.

Summary Questions

After every few new thoughts, *sum up* what you think you heard, giving momentum and credibility to the expressed ideas. Often, a client concurs with what I think is being said. But when there is a difference between what I understand and what the customer is saying, problems often begin to appear. It is vital to not let *your* beliefs and understandings of the problem areas get in the way of facilitating your customer's understanding of her situation.

I have found the best way to do this is by posing *summary questions* every three or four statements:

- Is what you are telling me . . . ?
- So what you're saying is that . . . ?
- Let me get this right. Are you saying . . . ?
- I'm going to sum up what I think you said, and I need you to tell me if I understand it correctly, okay?

Listen carefully to know when you are not totally understanding something. Sometimes you can be just plain confused. Or sometimes the words the other person uses leave too much room for individual interpretation and you cannot understand specifically what she means. During these times, I ask my most-used question: *Would you mind explaining that to me in a different way?*

Again, these questions are meant to facilitate, organize stored information, gather information, create rapport, and become part of the resolution process. Often, through the summation process itself, the disparity between the current situation and the desired one becomes clear.

This is an important point. It is here the reason for the person to buy becomes apparent. In my previous example, the summary question—"So now, with eight people, you know what's going on and can stay on top of everything you want to stay on top of, is that right?"—is a perfect example of my summary of what the prospect said and the self-evident nature of the problem. It isn't necessary for me to belabor the point. The prospect knows he must find a way to handle the situation.

It is vital that you understand what your client is saying and meaning, or not saying, or wants to say but cannot find the words for. Your job is to keep questioning until your customer feels comfortable that she is in the process of discovering a resolution *which may or may not include using your service or product.*

Differentiating Questions

Another set of questions come in handy for times when people are speaking in vague terms or generalities, using *always, never, everyone, sometimes, generally,* and *usually.* These are catch-all words which are rather dangerous in that each person can interpret them any way she wants to, making it possible to gloss over problems. *Differentiating questions* clarify meaning:

- Who, specifically? Do you really mean *everyone?*
- Every *single* person?
- When, specifically? Is it really *sometimes?*
- Does it *ever* change? Under what conditions?
- Under what conditions would it be different?
- Is it or was it ever different?

The more specificity the client can consider, the clearer her problem becomes.

Putting It All Together

Let's summarize the questioning process and how it works to gather information:

Inviting questions initiate the conversation, begin rapport-building, and start the customer speaking.

Facilitating questions begin the information-gathering process by extracting quality information which may be stored in an unsystematic fashion in the customer's consciousness and is difficult to access without assistance. These questions promote the exploration of the client's environment.

Specifying questions bring greater clarity to the newly emerging information. By asking *what,* they clarify each point and the emerging problem space.

Organizing questions focus the attention on the possible solution and how to accomplish it. It is here that the customer realizes the problem: there are often insufficient resources on hand to assist her in reaching her outcome.

Summary questions clarify understanding both you and your client.

Differentiating questions bring specificity to general statements (*always, everyone*) to clarify the points which need further examination. They are used as needed.

Old Model Questions

Since I had been trained for years on how to use "proper" questioning techniques, it was initially confusing for me when I realized that the questioning strategy I formulated—in itself very different from what I'd been taught—was far more successful in achieving bottom-line results and helping people get their problems solved. I took a long, hard look at what I call the *old line* questioning techniques and discovered why they weren't effective. Let me share that with you.

Open Questions

Sales courses continually teach people that they are supposed to use *open questions.* While there are many definitions of open questions, the one I will use is "questions which get the customer talking." They are questions such as:

- Are things going along well?
- What seems to be the problem?
- How do you think you'll solve the problem?

Open questions do not specify where you and your client are going, nor do they control the structure of the call. Open questions let the client's mind wander in and out of the problem, going anywhere she wants with her thoughts. In the end, you are both left more confused and the problems left ignored.

I'd like to throw in a fun example here. While running a seminar recently, I became ill with food poisoning and had to end the program early. Back in my hotel room, I bolted the door and spent a very uncomfortable afternoon lying on the floor. At one point, the housekeeper tried to enter. I yelled, "I'm sick. Please leave me alone."

She answered, "Is there anything I can get you?"

"Yes. Could you call my partner and tell him to fly up? How 'bout sending a doctor? I know: can you get me some medicine?"

The woman became exasperated. "I mean, like towels or sheets?"

She had asked me an Open question. Asking a Facilitating question like "Is there something you need from housekeeping?" would have been clearer for both of us.

You also cannot enhance your relationship with Open questions, as they do not build rapport. When someone asks me an Open question these days, I know she is not interested in helping me find a solution but only in getting the task of asking a question over with, or looking for a specific word, phrase, mistake, or idea to sell into. The task takes precedence over the relationship, and I lose trust in my questioner. Open questions are okay to use when the relationship is already well-established and conversations are light and informal, with no outcome other than relationship-building.

Leading Questions

Leading questions make people feel manipulated. A few examples are:

- You need to take a more detailed look at your policy, don't you?
- Your program really doesn't address all that it could, does it?
- Don't you think you could use . . . ?

In each of the above questions, the real message we are passing on as salespeople is "*I think.*" Any answer a client gives you is in the lose-lose category, since the answer is a set-up and is based on the seller's belief system. After all, these questions are structured around how *you* want to be answered. If she agrees with you, she must admit an error was made somewhere. If there is disagreement—either because the customer does not feel comfortable enough to admit an error, or because in fact she does not believe your statement *whether or not it is accurate*—then the person may be denying or unaware of a real need. The question leads the client into defending an indefensible position—and discomfort.

"Why" Questions

People are always amazed when I suggest that *"Why" questions* should not be asked. The information received is always a rationalization of behavior. All answers to these questions start with, "Because . . ." There is an automatic defense posture. If you approach the same issue by asking them, "What's important about . . . ", you get to the heart of the issue: values. Try asking someone why she is wearing what she has on today. Then ask her what is important to her about what she is wearing. Notice the difference in her answer to the second question as well as her thought process to find it. In order to answer the question, she will have to organize her experience, sift through possibilities, and make comparisons. Along the way, she will also come up with new observations about herself, her wardrobe, and her process of choice. "Why" will never get you there; it seeks only low-quality information.

Closed Questions

I understand that *Closed questions* have been given bad press. I'm not sure why. For me, asking a question which gets a "yes" or "no" furthers my information-gathering or facilitation process. It remains within the structure of the questioning process without deviating from the content and provides more information about this person.

There are two effective ways to use these questions: first, to gather specific information once rapport is established (such as when scheduling appointments or checking on a client's progress); and second, to remain in control of the structure of the call by establishing the content of the questioning process ("Do you use training programs?" or "Do you feel comfortable discussing the projects giving you problems now?").

I believe that, in the past, people attempted to use Open questions to keep people talking, and they found that Closed questions defeated that purpose. Since our questions are asked with a totally different outcome in mind, the old philosophy about Closed questions no longer applies.

In subsequent chapters, we will discuss using the questioning process for cold calls, referrals, prospecting, customer service, incoming calls, complaints, and follow-up.

In the next chapter, we will examine the questions we need to ask *ourselves* in order to understanding what the customer is telling us.

Skill Set 6b

Asking the proper questions

1. Begin listening to the questions you currently use during your business calls. After discovering the specific ones you rely on most, write them down. Put them in categories of when and with whom you use each type of question. Are there patterns? Do certain questions predominate? Under what conditions do you use each of them? Are some more comfortable than others?

2. Notice what types of responses you get from your current questions. Again, are there responses you get over and over again? Are these the responses you want? Do the questions get you different responses from different people? Can you categorize the responses?

3. Decide which questions provide the information and outcome you desire and which ones don't. Look at the techniques presented in this chapter and decide which techniques you will feel comfortable trying immediately. Put a list of them near where you make your phone calls and experiment until you have integrated them into your daily routine. Note the differences between information you receive from your initial set of questions and information you receive from the new ones. Does rapport shift? Do relationship issues change?

4. Each week, try some of the new questioning styles and techniques. Note which ones get you what you want. Give all of them at least a day's trial and note the responses you get. Should any of them cause you discomfort, find a replacement question which is similar in outcome. Be flexible. Keep a running log of your

new outcomes. Understand that there may be a discomfort level at first. That just means it's new.

5. Consciously note under what conditions you travel between Self, Other, and Observer. When is it harder? What percentage of a conversation do you stay in Self? We will examine Observer questions in the next chapter, but, for now, begin the process of becoming aware of how you do what you do. Start mentally pulling out of conversations at convenient times to check your level of rapport.

Questioning Ourselves

Chapter

7

How We Interpret Communication Clues

It is clear that an important relationship exists between the **content** and the **meta-message** of what we hear. Together, they make a whole. If they are separate, we understand only parts of the story. The most difficult part in applying these two concepts is knowing when to listen for either content or meta-message and how to access the information we need at the appropriate time.

Listening For The Meta-Message

My theories about the differences between the two concepts came about when I was learning how to listen effectively. During the period when I didn't understand the content of what people were telling me, both as a stockbroker and in my computer support company, I was constantly talking to myself, asking myself what this person was talking about, trying to find some way to make sense of it. Since I had no patterns of thought in these areas to begin with, I had no memories to compare against what I was hearing. Therefore, I had to be painstakingly aware of specific bits of information in order to find a way to stay with the conversation and know enough to ask reasonable questions. At the very least, I wanted to sound intelligent. What did I have to know in order to not get involved at the content level—which in those days I truly could not discuss in any intelligent fashion—and still know how to hold up my end of a conversation? The process I discovered is one that I now use regularly. It's a way of separating the parts of someone's conversation—voice, words, meaning, values, intent—and getting meanings and messages separate from what the stated message seems to be. Let's take a look at how it works.

Listening To The Voice

I first become aware of the person's voice. Is the tone friendly? Busy? Hostile? I notice through his voice whether he is comfortable or not, either with the subject matter or with me. I also ask myself: how does the volume change during the call? Is there stress at some points and not at others?

What do these signals mean? For me, the voice is my window, my way of "viewing" what is going on. Each shift in the client's tone, volume, and speed indicates a shift in his thinking at some level. I constantly become an Observer and ask myself what each shift and change means to our conversation and our "we space."

I become "light on my feet." Usually, *more* of anything (volume, speed, or hard or soft tone) means the conversation is touching on something important to the speaker: frustration (with me, himself, or the situation), excitement, annoyance, or defensiveness. I have come to know the difference between comfort (usually softer, breathier, lighter), discomfort (edgy, shorter sentences, more confusion, less clarity), annoyance (harder, clipped, louder, directive, quicker), and acceptance (slower, playfulness, joking and light conversation).

So long as you continually bump yourself out of listening for the content and become aware of your client's every voice shift, you can better understand his situation and thereby have more flexibility in terms of which questions to ask.

Listening To The Language Patterns

Along with the voice, I peripherally note speech patterns and language preferences. I usually notice language preferences only if they are so predominant that my rapport with my phone partner demands that I pay attention to them.

I notice if the person prefers to use words which are *visual* ("I see." or "I'll look at it"), *auditory* ("Sounds good to me" or "Listen, I'll discuss this with . . . "), or *kinesthetic* ("Feels okay" or "Let's touch base").

If it isn't clear early in the conversation which type of words he favors, I use neutral ones which will not offend. These are *understand, think, notice,* and *decide.*

Sometimes I notice idiosyncrasies about the person's speaking habits or map which need to be matched to enhance our rapport. Usually, these idiosyncrasies jump out at me, as when one client said, "I'm learning to play the guitar and I went to *watch* someone play last night." (Obviously a very visual person.)

Along the same lines, pick up buzz words which are specific to his company culture (*attitude, down time, right-size,* or *re-promise*). When these types of words get used frequently, I find a way to weave them in to my own speech patterns, making the conversation more comfortable. I must continually make mental checks for this, as the patterns would be lost if I only listened for content.

Alternating Between Content And Meta-Message

I alternate listening between content and meta-message, giving attention to content only to gather the appropriate information to phrase my next question and do rapport checks.

There are times when listening only for content is vital—when you need specific information to set up a program or draw up contracts, for example. But listen mainly for the meaning behind the message—the meta-message—during the initial stages of getting to know someone or qualifying them. You can always go back and ask your phone partner to repeat an aspect of the content which you need to more fully appreciate if you are getting confused, or if a specific point keeps coming up and you've missed the importance of it.

Listening for content alone keeps you locked in your Self position, without flexibility or perspective, defending each point separately, and losing the whole for the parts. By traveling between Self, Other, and Observer, you can maintain an overview of the interpersonal dynamics and the development of the conversation.

I use a content check to maintain an overview. This means I listen for a while to the content from the Self position—listening as if this were a friend of mine who was telling me a story—then, at the end of a sentence, a pause, or a light moment, I go to Observer a do a check for rapport. *I continually do rapport checks throughout a conversation.*, asking myself:

- Am I in rapport? Are our voices matched? Our criteria?
- How do I know we are in rapport? In a "we space"?
- Is my approach or voice creating and maintaining comfort?
- Am I speaking to this person as if I either know him or would like to? Or as if we were strangers and would always remain so?
- Am I curious?
- Am I in control of the context of the call through my questions?
- Am I entering into this person's reality sensitively?

There is often a vast difference between the words a person uses (the content) any hidden agenda (meta-message) he is working out of, and the behaviors he is exhibiting. Notice shifts in the story line, as well as language and rapport issues, as a way to keep a running check on how you're doing.

Using The Meta-Messages To Form Questions

Let me give you an example of listening for the meta-message. I recently called a major company and spoke with its training manager. After telling him my name and that I run communications skills courses, I asked him if he ran any similar trainings. He said they ran phone skills courses.

SDM: That's great. I teach that too. Could you tell me how your program works? [Here I am in initial agreement. I then give him the opportunity to think and speak about his program.]

Client: Sure. It's about an hour and a half and we go over telesales scripts. [This information tells me, at a meta-message level, that the company is interested in training, they are probably doing the best they know how, and they are pro-active in taking responsibility around increasing their bottom line. It also tells me the person is cautious about what he's going to hear. Other people might speak for two minutes here.]

SDM: Ah. Interesting. [I remain in rapport and agreement. This also gives him an opportunity to continue speaking. *Note here that it is now the prospect's turn to speak!*]

Client: What's yours like? [The prospect has chosen not to continue speaking about his program at a point when it would be typical for him to. However, he has also not defended his program. He is now showing wary interest in what I do, to see if there is a way his program can be improved. But I must be cautious, as it's very early in the conversation for him to be showing interest in what I do. This might be a set up.]

SDM: It's a bit different. We have a two day program. [I don't want this person to get defensive. I break down our differences into small pieces, as we have not established enough rapport for him to assimilate more. If I tell him too much too soon, I will lose credibility and getting back to agreement will be difficult. I also chose the time difference rather than the script element as a broad frame to start with. My main objective at this point is to give the conversation back to him. He cleverly got me speaking.]

Client: Two days? What do you teach in two days? [Obvious interest, with a bit of defensiveness creeping in with the curiosity.]

SDM: Well, it's probably real different than yours, but I would like to find out more of what you do. Is your course only for your salespeople? Or does everyone who uses the phone to talk to clients get trained up as well? [I avoid the trap of giving away too much information which the prospect could use against me if what I say makes him defensive. Therefore, I don't answer his question, but use the opportunity to become the questioner. I also ask two questions at once to make it more difficult for him to turn it around on me again. I heard his defensiveness and have backed down to make sure I retain rapport. I always get back into rapport by having the prospect do the talking. This gives me time to listen for, and ask questions about, potential problem areas which could be solved by adding further training to what they are already doing. If they don't use any training program at all, the process would be different still, as they would have to understand and want increased phone skills for themselves before they were even interested in what I had to offer.]

Client: Just the sales people. We don't have a program for anyone else, although I'm sure the secretaries could probably use one. [This person is getting cautious here. Not giving me lots of information, at a point when he could have talked for several minutes. However, he has admitted a potential further need.]

SDM: What's your success ratio? Do your salespeople get the sale or appointment they want with the script? [I'm taking a risk here that a direct question like this will not push him away. But he'll appreciate that I am playing the same game he is, and I am definitely asking him to put his money where his mouth is. He will respect me for this, as we are now in criterial rapport: we both understand the importance of the bottom line. Also, I ignored his comment about the secretaries needing further training. He already bought the idea for himself, and later in the conversation will ask me if the program would be appropriate for secretaries.]

Client: Well, it's just a numbers game anyway, isn't it? [Challenge, challenge. He's real curious about how I'll respond to this, and my response will make or break the "we space."]

SDM: Well, we work with relationship-building, so our outcomes are probably a bit different than yours. [He should get curious about this and wonder how I could be successful. At this point, he's also not defending his position too much, and since I told him several times how

different our programs were—and even our outcomes!—
he'll be willing to sit back and listen. But I must be careful
to preface everything with "The way *we* do it is . . . . What
we have found is . . . .]

By this time, the customer had discovered questions about
his own program and was ready to ask me questions about what
I teach. He noticed that the telesales training approach he used
was not working optimally and that the phone isn't just used for
sales. And that was only the first few minutes of the call. At this
point in the conversation, the customer was more interested in
what I had to offer—and in rethinking his approach and needs—
than when I began. But it was a difficult call. The prospect
continually attempted to get me into my old selling patterns and
had I done so, I would have lost an opportunity for potential
business. It's hard not to pitch when the opening seems to be
there.

Getting From Present Situation To Desired Goals

One of the reasons the questioning process is so vital is that
people are often unaware of the specific obstacles they will face
in getting from where they are to where they want to be. They
aren't fully aware of many of the issues they have left unattended
in the present situation. In big business, very few senior managers really have their fingers on the pulse of their staff. The reasons
for this are many. First of all, it is not the job of senior management to have direct access to the workers. They rely on their
management team to keep them informed. Secondly, many
workers and even supervisors do not tell the whole story to their
bosses. This comes from years of not being listened to or considered in times of change. It is always sad when I enter a company
as a consultant and meet with the workers alone. They spill their
guts, they cry, they become angry. And when I bring their stories
to management, I am told, "They are using you to get to me," or
"They have a hidden agenda. They are not telling you the truth."
The times I have succeeded in getting senior management to sit
down with their people and listen, I watch them take in the

information and begin to reconsider decisions.

But on the phone, during a sales call, I cannot do that. I have only the questioning process to assist managers in finding answers or sometimes just finding questions. It's easy to talk about the company's future plans and changes. But many managers have not taken the time to examine in detail where they are right now, what issues they face, what resources they need, or what evidence they will need to know that the desired goals are reachable. Discrepancies between the present situation and the future situation mean there is some type of problem that will eventually have to be addressed.

This process is easy to see from the outside when you are selling to large companies. But even if you are using the phone to sell vacuum cleaners, you want to know the present situation. Is there a vacuum already in the house? Have there been problems? Under what conditions would they need another?

I recently got a phone solicitation call from an organization to which I regularly contribute.

> *Seller:* Mrs. Morgen? Good evening. [By now I am ready to hang up. She used an improper way to address me, it's 8:00 at night, and I don't even know who she is.]
>
> *SDM:* Yes?
>
> *Seller:* My name is Mary from ABC. As you may know, during these trying times . . .
>
> *SDM:* Do you want money? Why are you calling? If you weren't from ABC I would have hung up by now.
>
> *Seller:* Um, yes. Your membership is due.
>
> *SDM:* Why didn't you tell me that to begin with? How much do you want? [I was prepared to give $250.]
>
> *Seller:* The annual fee is $50. Can I put you down for at least that amount?
>
> *SDM:* Sure. Anything else?
>
> *Seller:* No. That will be all. Thanks for your time. I'll send this information to you.

If Mary had brought me from the present to desired state, the conversation could have gone like this:

Facilitator: Hello. My name is Mary Senter from ABC. I know it's late in the evening, but is this a good time to speak for a minute or so?

SDM: Sure.

Facilitator: Did you know that your membership has expired?

SDM: No.

Facilitator: Are you willing to renew for another year?

SDM: Certainly.

Facilitator: Are you having any thoughts about the level of contribution you are willing to make? I could let you know what we are doing with the contributions this year if that will help you in making a decision.

SDM: I'd love to hear how you are spending the money.

Using these questions, the phone solicitor would have been able to get a larger contribution from me than the nominal fee.

Let's take a second look at some of the types of facilitating questions that will help you reach an understanding of a client's present situation:

- *causes*   "What makes you . . . "
                  "Under what conditions . . . "
                  "How do you do that?"
                  "How did you make that decision?"
- *specifics*   "What do you mean by . . . "
                  "Who/what are you referring to?"
                  "When does this happen?"
                  "Can you give me an example?"
- *values*   "What's important to you about . . . "
                  "How is that important?"

These questions will bring you to:

- *obstacles*   "What stops you?"
                  "What happens when...?"
                  "What would happen if you do/don't?"

- *effects*   "What does that get you?"
                   "What will this do for you?"

And finally to:

- *resources*   "What do you need in order to ... "
                   "How will you achieve that?"
                   "What plans do you have for that?"

The area least addressed is:

- *evidence*   "How do you know?"
                   "How will you know when ... "

Customers are comfortable discussing their future. They talk about what needs to happen and what it will look like when they are successful. They often embark on getting there, and find they are constantly fighting fires. What you can learn, as a buying facilitator, is that the difference between "here" and "there" includes minefields of issues that are not laid to rest and are exacerbated with change and movement. The sale is made at the point where a client's needs become highlighted, in the area where there is a resource need, and where minefields will explode unless defused. And the person who assists the customer in finding this need is the person who makes the sale.

Working With The Problem Space

As I learned to gather more and more appropriate information on the meta-message level, it became easier to ask questions which would help the customer discover his problem. The questions I asked myself were:

- Is this person aware of a discrepancy between the present situation and a future need?
- Are my questions the best ones to elicit the information he needs to make a decision?
- Am I asking my organizing questions gently enough to allow this person the flexibility to examine the available or missing resources which might solve the problem?

In my past, as a salesperson who remained solely in Self, I wanted to help solve everyone's problems—with my service or product, of course. I had the answers. But it was difficult to learn to take myself out of the fray and offer no solutions, only a relationship and lots of questions to help my client solve his own problems.

One of the hardest lessons I've learned is to sit back and let each customer realize he might need outside support (either a product or a service) to solve his problem. As a result, at my first opportunity to make a suggestion, I usually suggest that my assistance be reduced to helping him help himself with his own internal resources. This offer takes the edge off of the defensive posture many companies take when acknowledging a problem with no ready solution.

A large insurance company wanted to add telephone skills to their full and busy repertoire of in-house course offerings. While the Training Manager said he wanted to hire me to train all the offices, he stated on several occasions how self-sufficient the company was and how good his trainers were. The meta-message was obvious to me: he really didn't want to hire from an outside agency and in fact had been dragging his heels getting back to me on what he claimed was a priority issue. I put those observations in my head and played the game of putting together a proposal. I also included the price and program to train his own trainers, rather than my doing it. He was ecstatic over the idea, and we worked that around for some time. It soon became apparent to him that his trainers could not be freed up within eight to twelve months, and he wanted this program completed by that time. When he recognized, through my questions, that he had a time and content criterion which was more important than one of self-sufficiency, he hired my company to do the training. His final decision was made comfortably, with few problems. He had made the decision himself, although I knew right from the beginning that his problem space included insufficient resources. But it wasn't about *my* knowing it. *He* had to know it.

What To Ask Yourself When It's Not Working

During every phone conversation, do a check every few minutes to ask:

- Am I disassociating regularly to keep a continual check on my internal state?
- Are we in rapport?
- Are we in agreement?
- What do I need to say to remain in agreement?

My job is to be in relationship with whoever is on the phone. In order to have a "we space," we must be in rapport. If I recognize that there is a problem, I must take steps to discover what the specific problem is and how to rectify it.

The first thing that tells me my phone partner and I are out of sync is a physiological response I get to stress--a knot in my stomach. For years, I used to walk around my work environments with this knot, not recognizing when it began and certainly having no idea how to get rid of it. I have since learned that when I am out of rapport with my environment (and this could mean the person I am speaking with), the pain begins. So when I am on the phone, and I feel a stomach ache, I go into Observer position and "take a look" at what I missed while in Self. At my earliest convenience, I make absolutely certain that I am in voice rapport, as this change alone will assist me in getting back immediately some comfort level with my phone partner. Usually I ask a question, as soon as it is an appropriate response to something the other person has said. This keeps the other person speaking and gives me time to assess the situation.

From the Observer position, I first listen for stress in my phone partner's voice, although by the time I have gotten back into voice rapport—which was most probably gone in order for us to have been out of rapport—the problem has been somewhat mitigated. If I've been quick, I have caught the situation just as it changes from comfortable to uncomfortable. I ask myself what took place between us at that juncture:

- Was I in Self only?
- Did I say something from such an associated place that I made the other person defensive?
- Did the customer realize something which made him begin to think of the problem differently?

I also take an inventory of the following:

- How well are our voices matched?
- How were our voices when I noticed the problem, specifically in terms of tempo and volume?
- Is my phone partner now using words differently than before? Are his words clipped, authoritarian? Does he seem to have a different attitude toward me?
- Is my phone partner speaking with the same level of comfort as before? What are the differences?

Once I discover what is different than before, I can begin to make educated guesses as to the cause. When a noticeable change in rapport occurs during an otherwise amiable or comfortable conversation, there is about a ninety percent chance that I moved out of my Observer, Self, and Other adaptation, and lost my ability to be impartial. From years of monitoring my own behavior during conversations, I find that when I lose my impartiality I go directly into Self. From Self, I **judge** ("That certainly is not the most effective approach to that problem, is it!"), **preach** ("But if you'd done it the way I suggested during our last conversation, you probably wouldn't be having this problem now"), **know all the answers** ("I hear that you think you are employing the most effective solution, but I've had many years in this field, and I *know* there are more effective ways than the one you have chosen"), **ask loaded questions** ("Don't you think that if it was going to work the way you had hoped that it would have done so already?"), and/or **comment inappropriately** ("You don't really do *that*, do you?").

Not surprisingly, using any one of the above approaches will quickly get me out of rapport, impair the trust and the "we space" we've built up, and put us in a place of disagreement which may or may not be retrievable. Since I believe it is the person who wants something from the call who must take responsibility for it, then it is my responsibility to undo what I did, if at all possible.

An example of this happened with a prospective customer who clearly had a staff problem. He was relatively open to exploring different avenues of assistance and we were having a constructive conversation. Suddenly I found my stomach knotting up in the old familiar way. I heard the man get "short" with me using clipped, loud words which were quite different from the earlier part of our conversation. I quickly got into voice rapport, which I had dropped when we were in criterial rapport, and asked him to explain more fully what he was speaking of. While he did this, his voice started to come down a bit, and I had a chance to go over the earlier part of the conversation. Here's how it went:

> *SDM:* What did you do when you sat down to speak with him?
> *Manager:* I gave him some much-needed advice.
> *SDM: What I would probably have done in that situation would have been to ask him lots of questions about his motives.* (Aggressive, disagreement)
> *Manager:* How do you know I didn't do that? You weren't there. You don't even know him. (Defensive)

It was obvious what happened. Given my highly valued criterion about someone giving advice without asking questions, *a criterion which I violated myself in this instance,* I immediately went into defense mode. I was in Self and associated when I offered to teach my phone partner his faults. Needless to say, he responded appropriately.

I removed myself from the call for a few seconds and asked him to fill me in a bit on this person (the most direct response to his annoyance at the content level), I was able to get back into my Observer mode, disassociate, and take stock of the situation. The person had not hung up. He was still willing to discuss his problem with me, albeit unhappily. I therefore felt the gaff was not irreparable. When he finished the explanation I had asked for, I softened my voice, indicating humility, and apologized.

SDM: By the way, if I could cut into the conversation for a moment, I just thought about what I said to you a few moments ago. You are right about me not knowing this person. I reacted to hearing you say you gave advice, and that generally goes against what I believe in for good communication. But that was exactly what I did to you in response, and you have every right to be annoyed with me for jumping at you like that. It goes to show what happens when I *assume* without asking questions. Please accept my apology.

The man calmed down immediately and said he hadn't even realized that I had done that. He was grateful for the opportunity to take notice of his own behavior when someone had done the same thing to him. He laughed and accepted my apology, and we were back in a "we space." I believe that he hadn't realized on a conscious level what had happened. He would have remembered the negative tone and attitude of the call before he remembered the content after we had hung up. But with an apology and a direct dissection of what had gone on, there was not only no harm done, but the relationship took a step forward. As I have stated throughout this book, my job is not to be right, it's to be in relationship. Using questions to guide myself and my phone partner through the maze of relationship and business issues, I help him discover his own problems and solutions.

Skill Set 7

Asking yourself the proper questions

1. Think of situations when you regularly disassociate and become the Observer. It may be while you are driving a car and notice the car ahead of you doing something you don't like. Or it might be while you are deciding how to discipline your child. Break down the techniques you use to bring yourself to the Observer position. Do you ask yourself internal questions to help you disassociate?

2. Begin to notice if you speak to yourself during a call. At what points during the conversation do you do this? What questions do you ask? Does the internal questioning process aid your call, interrupt it, or get in the way? How?

3. Note the specific questions you ask yourself most often during phone calls. Note which ones are used most often and under what conditions you are most likely to use them.

4. Start being aware of the rapport with your phone partner and specifically what you do to maintain it. Keep a check on the words, tone, comfort level, problem space, shifts in conversation, curiosity level, and differences between content and meta-message.

5. How difficult do you find it to speak to your phone partner and ask questions of yourself simultaneously? Do you lose the thread of the conversation? If so, how or when do you get it back?

6. Are you aware of having an internal dialogue which is subconscious and undirected? If you do, whether subconsciously or consciously, how would it be possible for you to have a greater awareness of what you are saying to yourself? Note the patterns which emerge.

7. Pick five questions from this chapter which you believe will enhance your ability to build relationships on the phone. Begin to use them as part of your internal dialogue process. Note any changes, both in your end of the conversation and with your phone partner.

8. Each day, or each week, add another question or group of questions to your internal dialogue. In your journal, keep track of the differences when using these questions.

9. Begin to analyze conversations and how they flow during the call in terms of:

- Voice fluctuations in speed, volume, and tone.
- Levels of stress or comfort. Is the conversation loud or soft, fast or slow? Does it include shorter words or longer words, severity or humor?
- Admission and discussion of possible problem space.
- Willingness to answer and ask questions.
- Level of trust and rapport evident in the amount of information shared.

10. If there doesn't seem to be a change in the type or quality of conversations you are having, given the use of the new questions, what do you think would make a difference?

Listening

I am always amazed when listening to business conversations and hear salespeople go into long monologues. They should be listening. I've often heard it said that a salesperson should listen and speak in the same ratio as her ears to her mouth (2:1). I think that's pretty rigid, and it does not take into account what is occurring within the "we space"—but the axiom is closer than not.

We forget most of what we hear within minutes of a conversation, so it is pointless to spend time on details which our customers will forget. We can enhance their memory by only speaking on subjects which already interest them.

A client's favorite topic is herself, and if you are doing most of the talking, you are not matching your client and are out of rapport, unless you have already established a relationship with her.

Since you are the one who wants something from the calls you place, you are responsible for creating what you want. Therefore, you must get the other person talking with you in a way that will match the "we space" you wish to create and the environment in which to discuss and discover needs.

When I align myself with the needs of my phone partner, I can direct the conversation to expand her perspective of all the issues involved. I take in the information being offered, internally compare it with what I know about similar situations, get curious as to how the customer or prospect plans to solve the emerging problems, and ask the appropriate questions to help her better understand the difference between where she is and where she wants to be.

If a client believes everything she says will be used as part of your sales pitch, she will begin to either screen what she shares with you, stop speaking with you, or not tell you the truth. If, however, she feels her specific needs AS SHE UNDERSTANDS THEM are being respected and supported, and does not feel she has to defend her current situation, she will buy from you what she needs. That is not to say that a customer always knows what she needs at a conscious level, but if you begin by telling her what *you think* she needs, she will defend her prevailing decisions without getting the opportunity to re-examine additional resource needs.

Reasons To Listen

Questioning and listening skills are the most powerful tools we have to direct a call. The two are closely intertwined, and it is difficult to isolate either of them. Our questions can lead a client from an examination of her current status to the environment she will be supporting should she choose to make a change. We must have acute listening skills to gather the appropriate information, frame appropriate questions, and heed the warning signs when we are getting out of rapport. In this chapter, we will direct our attention on the listening process.

Gather Knowledge You Don't Possess

I began learning how to listen appropriately when starting my computer software support company. I found myself in the unique position of starting a company in which I had no expertise whatsoever. As I believed in structure versus content, it never occurred to me that not knowing a thing about computers would hamper me. It didn't. But I had to learn to listen.

My company sold a service which involved hiring out skilled

people to solve computer environment problems. I understood the "people" end: the support I offered would save a company personnel, computer time, and commensurate money, free up the company's staff to branch out and get involved with projects more creative for them, and do projects which they did not have the personnel to take on or complete. That much I understood about computer support. But I didn't understand the technical conversations about hardware, computer languages or systems, or the environmental makeup of staff. These conversations put me into a panic until I learned to admit my ignorance and listen acutely to make my own sense of the words and concepts I didn't understand. Then I asked questions to assist me in understanding.

My initial attempts at making phone contacts for my support service were scary. At the outset, I only had to introduce myself and my company. Since I was offering a unique product, the more I talked, the more questions were asked of me--questions I didn't know how to answer intelligently. It didn't take long before I had to stop talking and be honest. I'd say something like, "I hope you'll forgive me, but I'm in the people business and computers are new to me. Would you mind explaining what it is you do or have problems with in a way in which a computer illiterate like me would understand?" I felt a lot safer asking questions and listening for responses which would assist me in asking other questions. I let the person on the other end do all the talking so I didn't appear so stupid.

This brought amazing results. People began to open up, and they patiently explained each part of their environment to me. Whenever I didn't understand a piece of what they were saying I'd interrupt, saying, "I'm getting lost here. Could you say that last part in a different way?" Every few sentences I would sum up what I understood to be true: "Let me see if I got this right. What you said was . . . " What I didn't realize at the time was that I was setting up a perfect rapport-building, trusting relationship by remaining curious and supportive, asking them questions which would lead them to organize their thoughts around how their environment was set up, remaining in agreement, sharing a "we space," and listening and speaking only to ask more questions.

My client controlled the content of the call (although I controlled the structure through my questions) and always felt in charge. Clients never minded talking to me as a "salesperson," because I didn't try to sell them anything. How could I sell them something if I didn't really understand how my services might interest them? Together, we examined their environment *in relation to my services.* Just by listening and asking the questions which came out of my real curiosity and inability to speak in any intelligent fashion, each customer assisted me in figuring out if my company could provide anything which would make her job easier, better, or more profitable. In other words, the selling was being done for me.

In a short time, I began learning about the technical environment, and, without realizing it, began falling back into my old ways with statements like: "I know what's needed," "I know what's best for you," or "I have the answer. Use my service and your business will gain time and money." It took about a month before I noticed my business falling off. I didn't know if it was the season or the economy. I never considered it was me.

One day I got a call from the Manager of Information Services in a company I had cold-called months before, asking them to hire us to do a big job. I had placed the chart in the dead file. While I gathered information about the job he needed us to do, he commented, "When we began having problems, I remembered our conversation. I remembered telling you about our plans for hiring and reorganization. You were real supportive, and we both agreed I didn't need help. But all the plans have gotten stuck somewhere, and now I need you. Can you help?"

I was amazed that a person I believed I had nothing to sell to had called me, wanting to buy. But I didn't DO anything—or did I?

This incident made me realize that my job was potentially much easier than I had imagined. *This was the first time I realized I have nothing to sell unless my client has something to buy,* and that the whole process was independent of how much I believed she needed to buy and how inventive, persuasive, or compelling my sales technique was.

Choose The Cues To Frame The Questions

Once I became fairly intelligent about the technical environment, it became hard for me to be really curious. My initial curiosity had been based on ignorance and a need to understand content. Now I had to learn to listen in a new way; not for environmental content, but for cues on which to base my questions. My job was to direct my client's thinking toward discovering discrepancies between her resources on hand and ones she would need to solve her future problems. To do this, I had to concentrate not only on *what* the client was saying, but *how*, as she would initially speak to me as an outsider and defend her environment rather than use the opportunity to explore it.

Listen For The Meta-Message

Listening not only to words, but the *way* they were said and emphasized gave me insight into stress areas, problems, and uncertainties. The *whys* behind the words were also of interest. Was the customer open to exploring problems or did she want only to get agreement for things being fine the way they were? Did the person want to share information with me, or keep it from me?

When people speak, they generally choose words which move their thoughts in a direction toward some goal. Facts build to a conclusion through a zigzag of details and explanations. Descriptions paint a picture through a circuitous route. Problems emerge when the present situation is explored en route to an explanation of the desired situation. By listening to the actual words the speaker chooses to define her thinking, I can make determinations as to the person's meta-message.

By listening for the meta-message, I can often redefine words. For example, a statement such as, "The guy is a **systems man**" tells me the man is an analyzer, won't make a decision quickly, and probably has difficulty building relationships. When someone says, "I'll get to it as soon as I can," I know that there's no urgency. "We haven't looked at that problem yet" usually means this person is not committed to creating a change. Issues that are not high priority may be pinpointed by, "We have to be aware of the budget." My belief is that *language is only a representation of*

what the person is experiencing. If I get caught up in the language—
or the content—then I miss the experience itself. To focus on the
message behind the message, I must continually ask myself:

- What does this mean? What is this person really saying?
- Is this person aware of the discrepancy between the present
  situation and a future need?
- How can I help this person examine this area?
- What questions must I ask in order to assist this person in
  understanding the problem space? In getting from present
  state to desired outcome? In examining available resources
  which would solve the problem?

Talking Versus Listening

During any moment in a conversation, I can only either talk
or listen. During the times when I have an internal dialogue,
which I do from Observer, I am not able to fully hear the other
person and a portion of the call doesn't register. Since some of the
content gets missed, it's important to know specifically what to
remember about each conversation. Pay special attention to:

- the *call outcome* based on the relationship or "we space" you
  and your client are developing
- the *progression of the relationship* to include trust
- the continual *emergence of new facts* (time frames, politics,
  staff shifts, product developments, and budgetary
  complications)
- *follow-up* activity, promises, responsibilities
- how you will handle the problems.

Relationship and rapport issues are at least as important as
specific details. The feeling your client is left with at the end of
each call is important since she won't remember many of the
details anyway. Answer the following questions after each call.
In the notes you take about the contact, record any patterns in the
answers. Then when you place follow-up calls, you will have the
information needed to quickly get into rapport.

- Is there a budding or continuing business relationship? Or enough only to ask for a referral? Or will the chart go in the "dead" file?
- Was it easy or difficult to have a conversation with this person?
- Was the rapport tenuous?
- What information about the client's verbal or voice patterns should be kept in mind for future calls (strong visual language patterns, no sense of humor, preference for brusque, quick conversations, etc.)
- Was there agreement? Trust?

Read The Clues

Listening for content gives me the issues the person is willing to let me know about. Listening for the meta-message gives me the underlying problems the person faces. Here's a clear example of the difference.

I recently got a call from a company which was "having a look at improving the service of two call groups handling customer service calls" (content). The meta-message was that they were somehow less than happy with the service their people were giving. I was given the name of a man who headed up a committee which was organized to "see if there was a viable way to make some improvements" (content). The meta-message here reads, "see if it would be cost-effective to make the system more efficient." After speaking with the man, I found him to be interested only in phone lines, minutes per call, repeat calls—that is, systems, not people. When I pointed this out to him, he said his people had the information to handle the calls appropriately and that the problems would be solved by checking on the information level of the call-handlers (systems again) but mostly by improving phone lines (content). The meta-message was that this man did not want to deal with relationship issues. I called the senior manager back, told him that his man was not interested in addressing the problem through relationship means (this problem had remained unstated at the content level until I addressed it here) and that I could refer him to someone in my field who could deal with systems. My phone partner became annoyed and the real issues finally came out: "I am no longer willing to put up with what this approach has been costing me in lost revenue, unhappy customers, and high staff turnover. I put him on a committee with relationship-oriented people and they'll all decide together what is to be done. Send your proposal on what you think needs to be done and I will get it to the committee in time for their next meeting."

At the meta-message level, the difference between the present situation and the desired was obvious: there was a people-problem which had not been dealt with. There appeared to be a hidden agenda going on, as well as the problem of seeking a solution to a people problem through a systems approach. ("Get the committee to fix it!") In my map, there was a mess which probably wouldn't be solved easily, as there was little respectful communication going on within the company. On a structural level, I remained cautious as to where I would fit in, as I had no reason to believe I would be treated any differently than the internal people.

If I remained on the content level in this instance, this level of interpretation would have been lost. It would have sounded promising: here's a company with a problem. The senior manager himself called me to involve me in fixing it. He was committed to fixing the problem, wanted me to go in and fix it, and would have helped me to do the job. I know lots of sales people who would see the dynamics as such. Then they'd wonder how they got involved in a messy situation which ultimately, in all likelihood, would not end up as an assignment.

In another instance, I went to visit a potential client who needed a training program for seven divisions of a multi-national insurance company. He was cordial, bright, and interested, and on a content level, said all the right things flawlessly. He was to follow up on several items and give me dates. He had an agenda which he followed. Oh, he was efficient! But he was the only company person at the meeting! If the task were as big as he said, there would have been a lot more people: middle managers, training staff, department heads. The meta-message was that the man was not going to do any of the follow-up and was just performing an exercise in importance.

Know What You Need To Know

The structural questions I ask myself concerning the specifics and the problem state of my client are:

- What is this person's job? Her environment, company politics, areas of responsibility, budget-wielding power?
- Are her considerations mainly cost, time, or quality? Task or relationship?
- Is this person the decision-maker?
- Why is this person taking time to speak to me?

Get Into Rapport

I get the answers to my questions by listening to the customer throughout several conversations; through a gut reaction from her voice tone (is it supercilious, friendly, open, curt, or egotistical?); through a willingness or unwillingness to look at her environment with its good as well as bad points; and through the relationship-building process. What I find, consistently, is that the more fully developed the rapport between us becomes, the more honestly and comfortably we can look together at needs she might have, by going from agreement to agreement.

Conversations become complex, however. I listen for content, then listen for structure and meta-messages, frame questions appropriately, ascertain when to talk and when to listen, and remain in voice and criterial rapport. I go back and forth between being associated and disassociated, trying to make sense of the customer's environment while helping her do the same, and constantly monitoring for some level of agreement.

In the pages ahead, I have broken down the listening process in a step-by-step fashion. You should consciously learn and practice each step. Some steps may be familiar, as you may do many of these behaviors unconsciously. That's not to say learning the individual aspects of listening will be easy: listening usually involves unconscious patterns, and breaking them down to make changes is cumbersome. Yet without the ability to *choose* the listening patterns you need in any given situation, your communication will be hindered and your behaviors random. When it's not working, you may not know what to change to get a different result.

Aspects of content, such as responses, openings, closings, etc., will be discussed in Chapter 9, What to Say When it's Time to Talk.

I have included many of the concepts we've used throughout the book and have further expanded them around listening strategies. Following this chapter, we will be putting them all together—the questioning and listening, the associating and disassociating, the rapport and the relationship, moving from present situation to desired state—to apply them to your daily sales needs. If you are having trouble with any of the strategies in the book following this chapter, make sure to review that section before moving on.

The Four Types Of Listening

In my map of the world, I assume four basic types of listening, which I use consecutively. These are:

- listening with full attention for content and no internal dialogue (neutral, Self)
- listening with full attention for structure and meta-messages with partial internal dialogue to remain disassociated (Observer)
- listening with partial attention while comparing what the speaker is saying to my own internal references (Self, Observer)
- listening as an Observer to the whole process—the two-sided conversation occurring between me and another (Observer, Self, Other)

It's interesting to understand the consequences of each type of listening, as each affects the quality and amount of information I take in and the level of rapport I share with the other person. If I remain in Self throughout the call, my success will be directly proportional to only the similarities in the maps I naturally share with my phone partner (those calls where there is instant comfort or discomfort). If I remain in only Observer, I sound like a person making a sales call who is *trying* to find a comfort level with the client. (Did you ever get a call from a salesperson who sounded like a radio announcer?) If I remain in Other, I end up supporting the customer around her present state and not trying to find the missing resources. This is what happens when you hear sales-people do all of the right things: their clients and prospects love them and yet they have a low closing rate. So while we are listening, our ultimate goal is to travel between the three posi-tions in order to get all the pieces of the puzzle to fit.

How To Travel Between Self, Other And Observer

The best method I have found to create a successful call is to do lots of traveling between Self, Observer, and Other, as dis-cussed previously. Most of the time I act out of Self, using my own personality, voice and language structure. I occasionally use Other to check out how it feels to be having a conversation with "Sharon" from the other side of the phone. But the most impor-tant position I can take in order to ensure as much behavioral flexibility as possible is Observer. I have discovered an easy way to teach people how to get into Observer whenever they need a new choice.

From monitoring myself and working with many hundreds of course participants, I have discovered that people sit forward when they are associated and in Self, and lean back when disassociated and in Observer. When a negative or unsuccessful experience is occurring during a phone call, people are most often hunched forward over their desks, with their shoulders forward or scrunched up and heads down (in other words, in an unconscious incompetent state of associated/Self). Successful experiences seem to show people sitting/leaning back in the chair or standing, with torso and shoulders back and head up—in an unconscious competent state of disassociated/Observer. People generally shift back and forth during conversations, but it's the disassociated position which gives *choice*. Therefore, when you are having a conversation which is NOT working and you need a new choice, check your posture. Sitting back will put you in Observer.

Since in our daily lives we alternate between leaning forward and back, associated and disassociated, unconscious incompetence and unconscious competence, several times during any given conversation, I'm not certain why we seem to operate successfully during phone calls when in Observer and unsuccessfully when in Self. But give standing or sitting back in your chair a try. It works.

Here's a breakdown of how to use the three positions together during a conversation.

- Your personality, playfulness, and genuine caring come from Self.
- Fluctuations in voice, content, and language patterns are recognized through Observer but executed through Self.
- Listen to content and speak from Self.
- Formulate questions from Observer.
- Listen for meta-messages through Observer.
- Check on voice and criterial rapport through Observer.
- Gain an understanding of how to respond to your prospect by noting internal dialogue and historic comparisons from Observer.
- Formulate the next question with your newly-gathered information in Observer.
- Running checks on how you are being received come from Other.
- The relationship between you and my phone partner continues to flow and build trust (Other, Self).

Steps To Listening

Minimize Internal Dialogue

Remain internally neutral to get the different types of information available from the person's voice during the initial greeting. Have NO internal dialogue.

While preparing myself to take in as many initial impressions as possible, I work at keeping internal dialogue to a minimum so that I don't miss the subtle cues in my phone partner's voice inflection or vocabulary. In fact, I only take a second out of this portion of the call for any internal dialogue at all. I must make a quick judgement as to the tenor of the call and what aspects I have to take into consideration: is the person busy? In a bad mood? A difficult person? I work with the feelings I gather from what my client is saying and the way she is saying it (Other).

The Voice

Match the person's voice and initial greeting when you introduce yourself. Give your name, offer a very brief general comment about what you do, and ask if the person has time to speak. For example:

> *Client:* Hello!
> *SDM:* Hello! This is Sharon Drew Morgen! I'm a salesperson in the customer support end of the insurance industry. Is this an okay time for us to talk?

I first listen intently to the voice my client uses in the greeting, and I match it identically for tone, tempo, and volume in my own greeting. At this point, I have no internal dialogue. As I introduce myself, I let my intuition, with information from the greeting, dictate how I phrase my first request for information. My speech patterns alter with each conversation—they range from stiff and formal, hesitant, strong, soft but clear, playful, loud and brusque, to courteous or powerful. Sometimes I am surprised to find myself using a soft, hesitant voice in response to a blustery, fiery one, but I seem to know unconsciously what will get us into rapport. I've learned to trust my internal choice once I've matched the prospect's voice perfectly.

After your initial greeting and introduction, continue to match your prospect's voice until you have personal evidence that you are in criterial rapport, which may not be until several minutes into the conversation. It might be when the customer settles into answering your questions comfortably and with thoughtfulness. Sometimes I can feel the prospect shift from distrust to comfort when I begin summing up the information I've gathered after my initial Facilitating questions.

The Opening Question

After being given a go-ahead that it's a convenient time, **ask a general opening, Inviting question** about your area of interest to begin gathering data. ("Do you have computers?")

This opening question will serve many outcomes. It will:

- get the customer speaking right away
- let her know you are interested in partnering
- give her control over the call
- give her some stake in continuing a relationship with you
- let her know you are someone to be trusted

Make sure you ask your opening Inviting question with curiosity, not for your personal gain. Remember, you may be entering into a long-term relationship with this person. Make sure it is someone you want to work with and share your valuable time with.

Language Patterns

To maintain or enhance rapport, begin to **notice the sensory-based words or characteristic language patterns** your phone partner uses when she begins speaking.

If getting into rapport is difficult, you may find that it helps to use similar language patterns which match your prospect's favored words, sentence length, or sensory channel. (See "Listening To The Language Patterns," on pg. 97.) It may be that you never have to use this option. Just be aware of the times when it is obvious to you, and use the option appropriately.

Associate Into Content

Begin to listen for content from an associated place, as if you were listening to a friend with interest and concern.

After conjuring up a real or imagined picture of this person in your mind's eye, become associated into the *content* by listening to the opening sentences of your phone partner's end of the conversation.

Disassociate To Summarize

Disassociate and take a few moments (about three seconds) to **have an internal dialogue to summarize what you've understood so far.**

Take this time to make an internal note about your initial impressions of your client: is she open or closed? courteous, stiff, hostile or friendly? This gives you the tone—voice and demeanor—to use for your facilitating questions in the initial information gathering phase.

Getting Into Agreement

While still in voice rapport, **use your internal assessment to summarize your prospect's opening remarks.** Don't move on until you get agreement. When you do, your prospect will probably use the summary to become more trusting and to elaborate further. She will begin getting into criterial rapport if your summary is accurate and has moved the conversation along. But remain cautious. Continue using voice rapport until your second summation.

Facilitating Questions To Ascertain Present State

After your initial dialogue, begin asking your client Facilitating questions, with the type of curiosity you would feel with a friend. Use the information to begin building your representation of the prospect's present environment. When the prospect begins her response, go into Observer and listen for voice and language patterns to ensure continued rapport and congruency.

As mentioned, it is vital to get the other person to speak first. This provides the information on which to base your questions and answers, keeps you in control of the conversation, and draws a clearer the picture of the current situation. (It's impossible to spend too much time uncovering the complexities of a client's present situation.)

Assess Your Status

Begin to **direct your attention for the first time to the meta-message.** You will need lots of internal dialogue.

At this point, you should begin to get a more complete

understanding of what the call is about. Do the two of you have enough criterial rapport on which to base a continued conversation? Does she seem to be willing to enter into a "we space"? Do you have similar interests? What are the problems which have to be solved?

By going into Observer and listening to the ease with which you and your phone partner are speaking, you can keep a check on your level of rapport. By gauging her willingness or reluctance to speak with you, you can decide how detailed to make your questions, when to sum up, when to throw in a joke or story, or when to just say, "Oh, really?" to keep the prospect talking.

Continue asking Facilitating questions about her present state. Remember, you are posing questions to assist the client to discover her needs and either buy something from you or give you a referral.

Listen For Content

Listen to the content of your client's responses, first out of associated curiosity, then from a disassociated place, then to make sense of what you've heard.

Note the content and how it fits with what has already been shared, the voice tone and volume, and the person's continued willingness to speak.

Summarize

Regularly summarize what you hear. Do this every three or four sentences, or at the end of every logical thought sequence. It cements relationship and mutual trust.

Reassess The Conversation Through The Meta-Message

Continue to remain disassociated. **Keep an internal dialogue to constantly reassess all the pieces you are working with.** Use the data to gather to begin to frame your Specifying and Organizing questions.

A few minutes into the call, disassociate to ask yourself meta-message questions: what are this person's business goals? Values? How does she do what she does? What part of this conversation should I respond to? Are there any obvious language preferences? How does her voice fluctuate or change in volume, tone, and tempo? What is important for this person and needs to be addressed? What questions should I be asking? The longer she talks, the more time you have to ascertain her intent.

I find that unless I am gathering specific information on which to base calculations, I really don't have to listen to much of the content of a call once it is in progress. It's far more important to **understand the meta-message** during the call. It also gives me the amount of control I need.

Ultimately, your success hinges on your ability to disassociate and stay aware of the meta-message at all times.

Keep A Check

Take a moment every now and again to **check if you are in criterial rapport.** Is the other person still willing to continue speaking? Does the customer trust you enough to give you quality data and to use your interaction to actually explore her environment? What information are you picking up? Is a resource issue surfacing?

I do all of this very quickly, but I recommend a check-off sheet for you for the areas you would like to understand better.

Move Between The Call And The Caller

Continue listening for content, and continually **disassociate in order to gather the data necessary to phrase the next question.** Your questions should go from Facilitating to Organizing to Specifying. Continually sum up.

I spend the rest of the conversation going back and forth

- between Self, Other, and Observer
- through voice cues, mental pictures, and gut feelings
- between listening for content and asking structural questions around what skills are needed to continue.

Note Internal Responses

Notice if you get tense, agitated, and associated (usually when one of your beliefs has been stepped on). Disassociate by sitting back in your chair or standing up.

Check Other

It's not only important to know what information you can gather and the rapport level you are maintaining, but also to **check on how the customer sees you.** Every once in a while, put yourself in your phone partner's chair and ask yourself how you are doing.

Maintain The Rapport

Keep noticing the level of rapport and continue asking questions that will maintain the buying environment. Remember the three elements to any successful sale are RAPPORT, RAPPORT, and RAPPORT.

Do *not* get into solutions. Also, do not get into a sales pitch until the customer begins to ask *you* questions. (See Chapter 9, What To Say When It's Time To Talk, for sales pitches.) Use the data gathered to create as complete a picture as possible.

It's important to remain in criterial rapport, and not, for example, talk about your belief about a company's need for outside help when the customer has let you know her strong belief in self-sufficiency. Always be aware that you are driving the conversation through the questions you ask, and your criterion should always be focused on maintaining rapport, supporting your customer's exploration of her problem space, and remaining in relationship.

Interpret Data

Begin interpreting data, both internally and with your prospect. Listen carefully for any indications that you are out of rapport.

If you and the prospect have remained in the conversation until now, you are probably in a "we space." Both of you will begin getting enough information to move the conversation toward the resources needed for your client's desired state. In fact, it would have been apparent by now if your client had no needs. Don't move too quickly here, because if you lose control by getting into content or into a selling mode, you will lose a potential customer. She has trusted you enough to give you lots of data. Don't abuse her trust.

If you notice areas of discomfort, distrust, evasion, etc., stop and ask the prospect what's happening. She will give you what she needs to continue the process. For example, "I appreciate all of the information you are sharing with me. Are you feeling comfortable examining this further?"

Determine The Direction Of The Conversation

At this point, **take stock of the conversation to discern exactly where it is headed.** Are you moving toward the prospect asking you to visit? Does she want a detailed explanation? Don't be too quick to get an appointment until you are sure this is a qualified prospect, and she isn't qualified until she discovers she has a resource need.

Note when the conversation turns and the prospect begins asking *you* questions. Initially, she will base her questions on comparisons, comparing what you are saying to either what she said, what her needs are, or what she believes is true. Be careful not to step on her beliefs and values when you answer. Listen carefully to how these questions are posed. You will get much information about how she thinks through the meta-messages behind her questions. For example, a question like, "What are the price parameters on the product?" presupposes there is no relationship between price and environment.

Keep Rapport Checks Following Responses

Listen to ensure that your responses to questions maintain the rapport.

As long as a customer continues to return questions, you can assume you remain in rapport. Listen for "Aha" or "That's interesting." Also listen for voice shifts (to note any errors you may have made). I was once speaking with a prospect who said at least six times that he wanted to see my work to get a more complete understanding of what I do. When it became apparent that his schedule and my course schedule made it difficult to connect, I mistakenly suggested he try a pilot. He got quite annoyed (and rightly so; I stepped on his criteria and was out of rapport) and I heard his voice become much quicker and sterner than it had been during any point in the conversation. He felt I was doing a hard sell and not listening to him. I quickly countered with an apology for not remembering that he wanted to see me first, and he calmed down.

The Close Of The Initial Call
Notice when it is time to wind down the conversation.
When there is a high level of agreement and comfort between you, and shared stories and experiences about the use of your product, it's time to think about ending the call and moving on to the next phase.

Ask the prospect where she wants to go from there. Listen for discomfort, evasion, curiosity, or eagerness in her response.

If you have remained in a "we space" until now, you will both easily decide where to go from here. You will know if this is a qualified prospect or interested customer. If you are still not sure, ask: "I'm recognizing that we both realize a potential need which my product would address. Would you like to move forward in some way or do you have other issues to discuss with me?"

Remember, *a good salesperson, or buying facilitator, doesn't have to close.* A customer who recognizes she needs your product will buy. The beginning of the "buy" is working together to establish a modus operandi. If you push for a close, you will lose the rapport you have set up. Be patient. This is a long-term relationship.

What To Do When You Lose Rapport

I found that when rapport is high between me and my customer, I unconsciously navigate the distance between us by shifting points of view. However, when I sense discomfort creeping in—when I begin to shift in my seat, or change my voice tone and volume, or begin speaking to myself with annoyance— it's a clear indication that there has been a shift in the rapport. Since I must be in Self in order to feel physical discomfort where none existed before, I must disassociate in order to recognize what new choices I need to make. Then I can begin an internal dialogue of questions. What's happening in the conversation? What do I need to do? Are our voices matched? Our criteria?

Changing Perspectives

Time and time again, I find that a problem occurs because I am associated into the conversation, listening with the "I" filter and not appreciating how the customer perceives the situation.

A perfect example of this occurred with one of my salespeople. She was having a good conversation with a hospital director who needed phone skills training. He was apparently quite taken with our program, and the conversation was a lengthy one. He told my colleague that they were having a two-month sales training program but when that was completed, they could possibly begin a phone skills program. He asked her to send some information.

She responded, "I'll send you the phone skills material, but I think you should look at *our* sales training literature before you start your program. We don't believe there's such a thing as sales."

The conversation ended there rather abruptly (the prospective customer found a reason to quickly get off the phone). The saleswoman didn't understand what had happened, that she had imposed her own belief structure onto the director, and that she hadn't listened to him from a disassociated position. The man had already arranged a sales program—a *two month* program at that—and she told him he did it wrong.

If she had listened to the meta-message from a disassociated place, she would have known that his plans were already made, that he was willing to tack our program onto his, and that he already agreed that our phone skills program would be beneficial to his people. In seconds, she broke the rapport and made him defend an indefensible position.

Occasionally, I lose objectivity too, and "fog out," giving up my position of choice at an inappropriate time. This happens when I allow myself to take comments personally and let myself feel attacked. When I rush to defend myself, I am associated into the content of the call and have lost my objectivity. However, I can disassociate almost immediately, as I have given myself physical anchors as cues: when I hear my voice getting louder and my words faster, feel my breathing speed up, and notice a shift forward in my chair, I am speaking from the personal "I" and am responding to content.

Once I *notice* the shift in my own body language and voice, I am disassociated. I listen for an appropriate break in the conversation, then say something—just a brief comment, usually a request for the person to repeat what she has just said—as quickly as possible, using a voice match based first on the annoyed voice I am hearing, then switching subtly into her original rapport-oriented voice. This gets her talking and gives me time to listen (in Other) to both content and meta-message and find out what is happening for the customer. How badly have I damaged rapport? What does she need to hear form me to get it back? What are the areas of disagreement? How annoyed is the customer? Is trust broken? Is there an opening to find agreement?

One of the ways I can tell how badly rapport has been broken is by the length of time it takes the other person's voice to willingly meet mine (which is her original voice) in volume, tempo, and tone. Once she begins speaking again, I listen carefully for her tone to change from louder to gentler, from quicker to slower. I wait to notice a shift back into rapport and listen carefully to note if I hear annoyance, anger, dismissal, or acceptance.

Apologizing

Sometimes I find it necessary to admit to my customer that I've damaged our rapport. I must get the conversation back to a place where the problem and its solution belong to her. To apologize, I might say something like, "Boy, I really got into that conversation! I guess those ideas really rattle me," or "That really got me! I guess I have to think about that. Are you still speaking to me?" or "I really must have some issues about what you just said. But it's really not my business to comment as there is no way I could know all the facts. Please accept my apology." The words almost don't matter, so long as the client understands I am willing to change my defensive or attacking position to one of acceptance. My job is to admit my mistake as clearly as possible— or risk losing a potential customer. The customer has been in a "we space" also and was probably feeling as uncomfortable as I.

Bringing The Conversation Back

Once I have made my acknowledgment and listened for the other person's response, I usually then use humor to lighten up the conversation and take the heat off. Again, I match voice, (usually much softer in volume) and joke a bit about my quick reactions and how they get me into trouble, or something about my inappropriateness. The other person almost always responds by telling me it's okay, that they do similar things sometimes. I gently bring the conversation back to the issue we were discussing before my gaff. Here I listen intently to make sure my partner is with me and in rapport. Although I may momentarily lose rapport, and therefore control of a call, I never lose the understanding that the outcome of the call remains my responsibility.

If the rift cannot be closed, you will hear the prospect back down on needs, find additional internal resources she has magically remembered, or recall an immediate time constraint, causing her to end the call abruptly. My choices are to quietly say, "I understand," and ask where we go from here, or to say, "It seems you are so annoyed by what I said that you are uncomfortable continuing our conversation." Since the chances are good that you have already blown this call, you might as well pull out the stops. It's your only chance to go forward.

I find that the better I can listen, can "become" the other person, can accept and take on her feelings, and can acknowledge any mistakes I've made, the sooner I can get back into rapport. After all, if she hasn't hung up on me, we are still having a conversation.

Skill Set 8

How to listen

1. Following several conversations, annotate the different types of listening you have used from the four types mentioned in this chapter. (See "The Four Types Of Listening," on page 123.) Begin to look for patterns: Under what conditions do you use a particular type of listening? Is there one particular type you use predominately? Do you listen differently with people you know? Clients? Prospects? Are you able to make shifts in listening easier under certain circumstances and not in others?

2. Begin to think about the specific behaviors you use with each type of listening. Make notes on your phone partner's shifts in content or voice when you respond after listening in each way. For example, when I am listening to content only, I tend to begin to mentally, then verbally, compare my experiences rather than help the other person continue his or her train of thought. This leads to a different conversation than if I listen to content with no internal dialogue.

3. Once you have learned to recognize how and when you listen in each different way, begin to play with choice. Have an entire conversation (maybe with a friend, for practice) using each type of listening according to the timing suggested in this chapter. What happens in each instance? Is one easier or harder than another? What type of results does each give you?

4. Listen for differences in voice when you are speaking with someone. What information does a shift in volume, tempo, and tone give you about your relation-

ship with this person? Does your "voice match"—or mismatch—create a difference in the relationship? Can you hear what happens when you change your voice? Practice listening for the differences.

5. Practice being disassociated for context. You may want to put these questions near your phone as reminders:

- Who is this person I am speaking with? (age, position, noticeable personal/voice characteristics)
- How will this person best receive me in terms of voice, criteria, mood and approach? (formal, courteous, gentle, funny)
- Why is this person giving me her time on the phone? What is it she wants from me?
- How can I best keep this person feeling comfortable? (in rapport)
- How can I maintain curiosity without losing rapport?
- What do I listen for to notice any problems we are experiencing? (voice shifts, content shifts, language shifts)
- What clues is this person giving me which will help me recognize how I can best help her organize her experience (and thereby help them recognize problem areas)?

6. Practice shifting between Self, Other, and Observer during the day—either on the phone or with people you know well. Which position gives you the most trouble? Do you notice differences in the quality of your conversations when you shift positions?

7. Devote your attention to one aspect (say, Observer) for a ten-minute time span every few hours for a day. It's not necessary to practice over the phone and can be

learned just as easily if practiced during face-to-face conversations.

8. Notice instances when you are out of rapport with a friend. How do you get it back? Do you use your voice, or conversation content? How specifically does it happen?

9. Notice instances when you are out of rapport with clients. What specifically is happening to you during this time? Note when you are disassociated or associated, listening for content or meta-message. Note what happens to the conversation. Initially, use the approach you have always used to get it back. Then use the skills discussed in this chapter to get it back. Is there a difference?

Section Three

The Application

What To Say When It's Time To Talk

9

Until now, we have discussed what you should do, say, or ask when setting the stage for a "we space" and a potential business relationship. There comes a time, however, when it is your turn to speak about your product or service. While you should not spend a great deal of time talking, there is some information that you can share with your phone partner should it be requested and appropriate.

Before getting into the specifics of what to say, let me state that there are times when it is unnecessary to tell your story. If you discover that the person you are speaking with is fully committed to continuing his buying patterns with products or services other than yours, it is not necessary to waste your time talking about what you do. Remember, not everyone can be a client. You cannot create a buying relationship unless the client believes he needs your product or service. If he doesn't, get out of the conversation as early as possible but don't forget to ask for a referral—which he will be pleased to pass on if your questions have been well-received and rapport has developed. Further, keep this person's name on the mailing list. He may use you later if a problem arises or pass your material on to someone else.

There have been times when my phone partner requested that I go through my whole spiel, only to tell me he would not switch suppliers. I never understand whether he is waiting for me to say something specific which will make him switch, if I've made an error in rapport-building, or if he is just comparing my services and price with another supplier's. In any case, when I speak with someone who is genuinely satisfied with prior decisions they have made, I try not to spend much more time on the phone.

Many times, a person will tell me he is completely satisfied with the product or service already being provided. When I offer him a summation and repeat what I've heard conveyed about the level of satisfaction, he may then back down. Here's an example:

SDM: It really sounds as if you are well supplied. I'm impressed.
Client: Well, nothing is perfect.
SDM: Yes, but you have a well thought-out plan which seems to be working quite well. If all my prospective customers were as well-cared for as you, I wouldn't have a job.
Client: We've done a good job until now. But you may have something that would help us improve.

While speaking to a referred prospect recently, he told me he had never brought in outside training in all the years he'd been at his company. Our conversation went like this:

SDM: Then why would you consider bringing me on?
Client: Well, it would be hard for me, actually. You'd have to prove to me that you could do my job better than me.
SDM: But I can't. It sounds to me like you are doing a great job and I wouldn't even try to compete.
Client: I guess I didn't mean that literally. It's just that trainers try to come in here and tell me how to do what they *talk* about and what I do daily for a living. But I think I'd be willing to talk to you about your program, as we can always use training on helping us improve our skills. However, I need to sit down face-to-face with you before we discuss it further. Do you mind?

If I had attempted to tell this man what my programs were about any earlier than two weeks later over coffee, I would have blown the opportunity to work with him. It was vital that I understood his criteria around using outside training companies before attempting to speak with him.

You will find that when you have established rapport and all your questions have been asked and answered, when there is trust and a problem situation is becoming clear, it is *then* the customer wants to know who he is speaking with. Occasionally, this happens before the problem situation becomes clear, but usually not before rapport is established.

Until now, our focus has been on creating a buying environment in which your customer or prospect can feel enough trust to discuss his environment and resources, and, if appropriate, request your support. Let's now examine the actual words which will advance your relationship-building process.

Cold Calls And Referral Calls

For years I've heard that cold calls mean face-to-face visits, and that the phone is used only to make the appointment. But I've seen many salespeople use the phone with the intent of making an appointment, not a sale. In my map, seeing a prospect does not create a sale, nor does it qualify him better than the phone. You waste a lot of time visiting unqualified people that way. Visits are important and necessary, but when they cost you and your company an estimated $270 per visit in wasted time, resources, and travel, and you can use a visit to complete the sale with an already qualified prospect, it makes more sense to do the up-front work on the phone through cold calling.

During a recent sales course I was teaching, I asked a young salesman, who believed only in face-to-face sales, what his closing ratio was. He muttered a bit and finally admitted to under ten percent of his visits. In a full day of visiting, he sees five people (and that's stretching it). He spends about seven full days time seeing about thirty prospects a month, all to open no more than *two accounts*. In other words, he wastes one-and-a-half weeks each month seeing people he won't close! The young man got quite defensive when I pointed out these numbers to him and defiantly asked me what my closing percentage was. When I told him it was one hundred percent, he stated, "That's impossible!" I pointed out to him that I only visit potential clients when they are ready to buy and I use the phone as the qualifying tool.

The question I had this man ask himself was: *If I were to only make three new sales a month, and only three face-to-face visits to close them, would this person I am speaking with be one of the three people I would visit?* If the answer is "yes", then give the person a sales pitch. Otherwise, get off the phone and throw the number away, get a referral, call back in a year, write a note, or do *anything* except waste your time on continuing the sales process.

I give full-fledged sales pitches to only twenty percent of the people I speak with, and I hope to close half of those. I do not believe that just because I have a good product and I am a good salesperson that my phone partner is the right person to sell my product to, or that it's the right moment to give the pitch. Your time is valuable. Get on the phone and keep calling until you reach those people who are qualified, or ready, to buy your product

For some reason, people believe cold calls are different than other calls. In my own experience, I was afraid to speak with someone I didn't know, never saw, and could not envision. Once I learned to make a picture of the person, and changed my outcome from trying to sell them something to developing a "we space," I lost my fear of being rejected, feeling stupid, or not knowing the answer to a question. Interestingly, while not every person I speak with wants to do business with me, no one is ever rude or disrespectful. Because I come from a position of relationship-building and respect, I am spoken to in the same fashion.

When I do make "cold calls," my questions take a different form during the initial stages than calls to people I already do business with. While the intent is the same—to create an environment in which a "we space" can occur—the initial rapport-building is crucial and immediate.

Let's break down the specific steps involved in a cold call. I have added appropriate examples.

Introduction
- Say "hello" and give your name and a one sentence description of what you do in an easy to understand and possibly slightly provocative manner. Use an identical voice match.

Make sure you do not specifically say you are selling something because you aren't. You will go through a facilitation process wherein the person gets to discover if he needs to buy your product.

- Ask if it is a good time to speak.

It is imperative when asking this that your voice is matched to the other person's voice as identically as possible. Make it comfortable for him to speak with a stranger. Make certain you match the volume and tempo, although with a bit of hesitancy to let the prospect know he's in charge. Salespeople go wrong here when they ask if the person has time to speak in a voice which sounds like they have been asking that question all day. No one wants to talk to someone to whom they are just another number on a list.

If the prospect says it's a bad time to speak, keep your voice exactly matched, and ask for a better time to call back. If you try to speak quickly and use the abbreviated time to make a quick pitch, you are out of rapport and you will not be heard.

By getting into criterial rapport around time, the odds of getting a call-back time are great. I recently sat next to the CEO of a large bank while on a plane. When I spoke about my book, his comment was, "If they ever knew enough to ask for a convenient time to talk to me, I'd be glad to give it to them. I was just starting out myself once. But they just start talking and expect me to listen! I don't know them. I don't have the time. I eventually mumble something just to get them off the phone."

- Start asking questions immediately to get your customer engaged and thinking along the lines you would like the conversation to take.

Stay in voice rapport as well, especially if your product or service is one which people get bothered about a lot (stocks, insurance, telecommunications, for example).

Here's an example of the Introduction process thus far:

"Hi. My name is Jan Davis. I'm in the service end of the financial industry. [She is a stockbroker.] Do you have about four minutes to spare? [Don't specify what is it you will be speaking about. Let your customer ask. This gives you permission to speak a bit. Also, use a small number of minutes so the prospect—who undoubtedly already knows this is a sales call—isn't committing to more than a brief time period] That's right. I'm a stockbroker with XYZ Corporation. Do you have all of your investment needs taken care of? [There is an imbedded command here: if you don't have *all* of your needs met, you should speak with me.]

One of the hardest thing to do here is listen and not speak, especially when your phone partner is saying he needs just what you can give him. Continue your questions. Remember that your job is to create a "we space." *The details of what you are selling are important only in relation to the person's comfort level, trust, and needs.*

• **Don't use a script. That focuses you on a "task" and takes you out of rapport.**

Many programs teach telemarketers to use a script, or some sort of opening gambit which will arouse the interest of the stranger on the other end of the phone. The salespeople generally are taught to introduce themselves by name, then by company in glorified terms, and then give a brief statement of what they are selling. The prospective client typically may hang up on these people, as they will feel they are just the next name on a list and that the caller does not really care what their needs are.

I recommend that you open with the company definition ("I'm with ABC Telecommunications in the cellular phone division."). Mention the product or service you are selling later on, and only in direct response to the needs of your prospective client. Remember that you have nothing to sell if your prospect has nothing to buy! So leave behind the script, introduce yourself by name and a very few words about what you do, then launch into your questions. And listen to your client's response. Save the speaking until it is IT'S YOUR TURN TO SPEAK. Then you will know exactly how you fit into the client's criteria and what you should mention to this end.

If your prospect gives you a reason why he isn't interested in speaking with you and doesn't hang up, this is a signal to make another stab at rapport-building. Remember to use voice rapport.

On some cold calls, the prospect will tell you immediately that he is fully covered (or in some way doesn't need your product or service). Accept him for being honest. There is a chance that he is generally negative around salespeople. If you take the time to get into rapport, you might be able to begin the information-gathering process. This must be done delicately, and you face the possibility of being hung up on, but you would have been anyway. If you give this person a reason to defend against you, he will.

Here's an example of a successful introduction in this instance:

> "Hi. My name is John Smith and I sell cleaning services to people too busy to clean. [He's a vacuum cleaner salesman.] Is this a good time to speak for about three minutes? Oh. You have ALL the equipment you need? I'm impressed. If all my potential customers were so well cared for, I'd be out of business."
> [LEAVE THE CONVERSATION HERE]

Remember, conversations go A-B-A. Once you finish speaking, it is the other person's turn. You have set up a situation which is almost impossible to not address. Very few people have ALL the equipment or ALL the services taken care of. If they respond, "That's right. I do, " and hang up, throw the number away and go on to the next call. Sometimes the person will say, "Well, I don't know that I have *all* the equipment I need ... " and give you an opening. By the way, in this latter example, when the client decides to address your statement and not hang up, create the opportunity for him to continue speaking by saying, "Well, it sounds like you're pretty well set." Then let him further explain. Don't take this opportunity to jump in and sell.

The Meat Of The Conversation: The Initial Pitch

Once you have begun the questioning process and engaged the client in discovering his resource needs, the conversation will make a turn. He will begin asking you questions. Only then do you have license to speak.

The first phase of your speaking is in direct response to the stated needs and questions of the customer. On an initial call, do not speak too much. The prospect will not remember it. He will possibly want to receive information and speak with you after reviewing it. *I do not attempt to get an appointment until I have qualified this person, and this is usually after at least two calls.*

So what do you say when it is your turn to talk about your product or service? First of all, don't go through your entire repertoire of material.

• **Speak solely to your client's expressed areas of interest. Use the client's needs to formulate your pitch, not your own needs of selling your product.**

Only sell the product or service your prospect has shown a willingness to consider. Salespeople are so ready to sell what *they* want to sell that they ignore the information the client offers on what he wants to buy. He doesn't have the patience during a call to give the salesperson free reign to run a sales seminar. Don't run down the list of what you think is wonderful about what you are selling. Mention only those items which will be pertinent to your client.

Get to the point. If your client wants team-building, give him team-building. If team-building is not what you do, offer to refer him to a colleague who can help him. If you have a specific brand of widgets, and your phone partner either has one and does not want to switch brands, or clearly has no need of one, ask for a referral. Then ask if he would like to be on the mailing list. And hang up. You needn't discuss why your product is different unless the person asks you.

I have worked with many insurance brokers who decide they are going to sell a new life insurance product, for example, *before* they begin the conversation. They miss opportunities to sell other products, because their filters blot out offered information which doesn't run along the lines they want to hear. As discussed under

Cold Calls, base your monologue on addressing the point(s) of need expressed by your client, in respect to both his actual needs and his attached values. Omit information which is superfluous at this stage of the sales cycle, trusting that if it is relevant, the occasion will arise for you to make the product or service available.

When I was in the information-gathering process with one of my now long-standing clients, he stated he needed a customer service program for a group of reps who had been in the same job for over twenty years. Upon further questioning, I found out their work was done primarily on the phone, dealt with internal as well as external customers, was highly stressful, and involved problem-solving almost one hundred percent of the time. My sales pitch to them went as follows:

> "My work centers around helping people do consciously what they already do well. [Let's be honest here. If these people have been doing the same job for over twenty years, they will not take to some outsider coming in and telling them what to do. It is important that I acknowledge their expertise as part of their highly valued criteria.] I don't teach anyone to do things *my* way, I help them have conscious choice around that which they already do well unconsciously. In other words, if what they do works for them, they can learn to keep doing it but have conscious choice around the process so they can incorporate their successful behaviors into the times it *doesn't* work."

I went on to discuss how to do this from a relationship base, using the phone to establish rapport and problem solve. I *did not* discuss my team-building programs, my prospecting programs, or my business consulting expertise. Over time and with trust, I was offered work in all of the above areas, but only after I proved myself in one.

The content of your pitch will be slightly different for each call, although a pattern will emerge and you will find yourself repeating certain phrases over and over—but DON'T USE A

SCRIPT! What you need to remember will be available to you once you are used to creating conversations.

• **Check in with your client regularly to make sure you get agreement.**

During your sales pitch, touch base with your prospect every few sentences to check for interest and get agreement regularly. You can ask, "What do you think?" or "Are you following me?" Make sure he is following you, that he can ask questions during the breaks you have provided, and that he knows his understanding is important to you. Here you can answer questions or keep going, depending on the needs of your phone partner. Just make sure you maintain control of the call.

I have found that the first few times I check in, I get an "uh huh." By the third or fourth time, I get some questions. I carefully answer these in direct relation to my client's already-discovered needs (not the ones I may have pinpointed personally) and to the exact response my client asks for.

Many salespeople who use a script or whose sole intent is to say enough to get an appointment miss these interest checks. When prospects don't keep their appointments, salespeople get angry. What they miss is that the prospect is giving them the words they wanted to hear to get them off the phone, without any intention of honoring the meeting. One of the reasons to keep checking in during your pitch is to ensure your client is with you. If there is any doubt in your mind that you have lost this person, get back into voice rapport with a question matching the prospect's voice. ("Are you with me so far?" or "Is this interesting you?") Listen for congruence in his response.

If you have remained in rapport, he will most likely be honest with you. If not, you will notice an incongruency in the voice while the person lobs you off with a "sure, sure" type of response. When I feel a loss of interest at this point, I say it directly ("It sounds to me like I've lost you"). The prospect is surprisingly willing to let me know exactly what is going on.

• **Don't speak too much, too long, or cover too much ground on the initial call, unless it is one of those rare instances when everything clicks.**

Your prospects don't have enough invested in a relationship

with you to really listen to all of the intricacies of your product or service. The filters a prospect uses during an initial call are more geared toward defense rather than exploration or acceptance. Say just enough to meet your customer's stated environmental and conceptual criteria, and calibrate carefully to the response you are getting.

• **Use caution. Just because the prospect has begun initiating the questions doesn't mean you have a customer.**

Once I am involved in a question-and-answer period which has been initiated by my prospect, it is obvious there is an interest of some type. But at this point, I have no way of knowing what form this interest will take. After several questions, my prospective customer may begin to talk about how using my product or service may be beneficial, but it's only hypothetical chatter—he kind of tries it on for size. It's important that you don't get too pushy here, when the first tentative steps toward what is considered a "close" occur, instigated by the prospect himself. Think of this process as a "buying," not as a "selling." Let there be plenty of silences here, while the prospective buyer considers his questions and digests information.

It may be prudent here to also throw some of the questions back:

Client: How would you go about bringing that aboard?
SDM: How do you think it would work best?

Occasionally, a customer will ask questions that he has difficulty answering for himself. Direct his problem back at him; it's his, along with the solution. You can only be there for him in relation to his needs.

• **Tell success stories wherever applicable.**

I love to tell stories, especially when it puts me in a good light and someone else does the bragging for me. It gets the hard-sale aspect of a pitch on softer ground, and it gives the prospect another perspective, albeit one which I am imposing. I tell stories about how clients are using my services, or how a client might have had an initial problem and how we solved it. It's a metaphor for how this prospect and I work together, and the particular story is chosen carefully to illustrate a point. Usually, it's cause for a laugh, and I don't flinch at telling stories which make me look vulnerable. This enhances the personal end of working with me by buying my product. I am a fun person and like to work and sell through laughter where possible. Here's an example.

> *Client: How* do run your team-building courses?
> *SDM:* Actually, sometimes they run me. Do you want to hear a story?
> *Client:* Sure.
> *SDM:* I was once running this program where everybody was mad at everybody. I had arranged for all of these wonderful exercises and games, and no one got along well enough to participate. I threw out the prearranged syllabus, put two chairs in the middle of the room, and said, 'Okay. I've had enough. I'm tired of all the barbs and innuendos flying here. We're not going any further until we get rid of this tension. Let's get it all out. Who's going to be first.' And one by one, they took turns sitting in the chairs, inviting an adversary to come up and share the space with them, and work out their history. It took the morning, but by lunch the mood had changed. It was so effective that the manager has since put two chairs out- side his office, and when people are not getting along they go to the chairs, even in the middle of the day, and get the issue resolved. And the team has used their new skills to win the number one Team Award of their 35,000 person company.

This story gives the prospect a lot of information about my criterion in a team-building situation. He may or may not like it. But if not, we might as well know that up front as I only want to work with people with whom I can do the kind of work which supports my personal values around training.

One note of caution: sometimes it's prudent to wait until the second call to tell a prospect a story, in order to ensure we have reached the proper level of comfort and informality.

Handling Objections

When I train people in phone skills, I am invariably asked how I deal with objections. I honestly answer that I rarely get objections. If you are in rapport and only speaking around issues the prospect has told you are highly valued business criteria, you won't have to deal with objections. I have found, however, that objections occur when I am selling what *I* want to sell, instead of what my prospect wants to buy, or when I am out of criterial rapport. However, there are numerous instances when my product is, in fact, inappropriate for the prospect.

• If your prospect expresses non-acceptance or objections, listen respectfully from a disassociated place. Remember to use his buying patterns when you go back into the conversation to check and he will tell you directly what the issues are.

Once a prospect hears the meat of your pitch, he may find your product inappropriate for his environment, politics, budget, or time. **This is the reason you gave him the pitch to begin with—to ascertain if it is the right product for him.** If it's not, you save a wasted visit. Not every person you are calling is ready, willing, or able to buy your product. Get a clear representation of the issues involved, however. If you need to clarify some point of confusion, state what you are doing directly: "I hear that you believe my product does X. I'd like to clear that up, if I may."

If the product is not the right one for him, agree. "Given what you've just told me, you are right. This product will not do that for you."

Let the customer take over the conversation from there. When he doesn't have to defend his opinion, he may find another application for your product. It never fails to surprise me how a customer will find ways and reasons to buy once he is not feeling pressured. Sales is a constant battle for us to give up the control of the content of the sale and trust the "we space."

Another common reason for objection is that you didn't cover enough ground in your initial questioning strategies to ensure that all the information you and your client need to work from is on the table. Go back to your questioning strategy and go directly into the middle of the problem. It's a great opportunity to further the rapport you are building. For example:

SDM: Are you with me so far?
Client: Well, mostly. Except that given our budget issues now, it's a bad time for us to take on this kind of a commitment.
SDM: I didn't realize there was a crunch now. Is this something that has a time frame on it?
Client: Well, possibly. Our new year is coming up and usually we save the items we need during the last months of the year for the beginning of the new year so we can enter the year with a surplus.
SDM: Is the money consideration what would stop you from looking into the possibilities of my product?
Client: Well, possibly. I'm not sure how applicable it would be anyway.

• **When the prospect feels less than comfortable with either you or something you said, money is the first objection.**
I have rarely found that money is a real issue except in highly competitive environments where the exact product can be bought cheaper. In this environment, sell your personal service. If it's a product which needs no service, and your price is not competitive, you have only your personal rapport skills and questioning strategies to make the difference.

My clients and prospects have almost always managed to find money from some pocket or department when they need what I have. I had one consulting job where the client set up a meeting of people from across the country, issued agendas, and got my plane tickets for me *before remembering to ask me how much I was charging for the day.* When I was in my computer service business, I ran the most expensive outfit in the world for what I did. It created a niche market. When you are giving clients the service they deserve, and thereby working from a relationship base, they never mind paying more for it. Money should rarely, if ever, be an issue.

When money is really an issue, I can usually find a way to maintain flexibility: either sell the product in segments and help the customer build up to full capacity, or offer some service for free—like a follow-up service call, or a bit of training. When I was running my computer services company, whenever there was an empty spot in a course, I called around first to existing customers, then to prospects, to fill it for free. This went a long way toward good will. I used it as a selling tool before and during the actual sale, and I continue to use any relationship-oriented reason to maintain contact with both clients and prospects. This keeps me in their mind when a need arises that I can solve.

The people I train are always amazed at the directness of the questions I ask. They are even more amazed when my prospects answer. Working from a relationship base makes it all possible because of the trust which evolves very quickly—trust that I care about the client, not just about selling my product to him. When I feel there is rapport enough to ask direct or money-oriented questions, I get straight, honest answers.

Products Versus Services

Selling a service differs from selling a product in the amount of flexibility you have. For me, selling a service is easier. I can bring forth certain aspects of the service and leave out others. I can downplay one and focus on another. And I can bend the capacity of the service enough to invent new capabilities within the stated framework. I don't have that amount of freedom with a product. It's either a vacuum cleaner or it's not. If I am working for a larger conglomerate as a telemarketer, selling one item after regular business hours, my flexibility for creativity and innovation is almost nil. Then, I have nothing but my ability to maintain rapport to create the buying opportunity.

• **When selling a specific product, plan on making more cold calls with less face-to-face contact.**

While there is a great opportunity to create reasons to converse and question about a service, people will give you only a brief consideration when one product is involved, especially if it is a product which has been pitched on the phone for years. If this is your plight, the opening of your call must be perfect with immediate voice rapport and a provocative opening line. For example:

"My name is Sharon Drew Morgen. I know you're not going to believe this, but I am a vacuum cleaner sales person and if you have time I bet you might tell me you've got the greatest vacuum cleaner in the world already, right?"
(or)

"Hi. My name is Sharon Drew Morgen and this will probably be your fourth call today that you won't want to take because I'm a salesperson selling a new type of long distance phone service."
(or)

"Hi. My name is Sharon Drew Morgen and this is a sales call."

In each of the above instances, the openings are just provocative enough to get a possible response. The first opening asks the prospect to comment on the state of his current vacuum cleaner. The second acknowledges that I'm selling a service we all use and are rarely happy with but might create immediate interest with the word "new." And the last approach usually elicits the response, "What are you selling?" It is imperative to get into an exact voice rapport around tempo here; if you are calling people at home (an automatic imposition), you have little chance of success without at least that. *Do not use a long scripted pitch. You will lose the person immediately.*

• **If you are calling the prospect at home after hours, be respectful of his time constraints.**

If you *don't* get into immediate voice rapport (the tempo will give you a hint as to how busy the person is), you've lost the call by the time you say "hello." Imagine a man coming home from work, just getting in the door from a dreadful day, just greeting his kids, looking at his four-year-old's finger-painting while trying to get his coat off. And you call with, "Hello, Mr. Jones, and how are YOU this evening?" If you got into immediate rapport, the conversation would go like this:

Client: Hello!
SDM: Hello! You sound busy!
Client: I am. Who is this?

SDM: This is Sharon Drew Morgen and this is a sales call—at a bad time for you, it seems. What's a better time?

The person will either give you a time, which will give you permission to call back, or ask you what you are selling. If it's the latter, give a one-word answer and let the person determine whether or not he wants to speak with you. He may hang up or be rude, but he would have done this anyway. By letting him know you respect him, you have a much better opportunity of getting a chance to speak with him. And once you do get the opportunity, go immediately into your questioning, not your sales pitch. ("Could you tell me something about the vacuum cleaner you're currently using?")

Ending The Initial Call

Since I have a basic belief that I cannot convince anyone to buy anything they don't want or need, I do not work with traditional closing techniques. In fact, I will repeat here that I believe a good salesperson doesn't have to close—the client will just buy.

• **Give the client the control over how to end your connection.**

After you have summed up the entire conversation and asked if you've gotten it right, let your prospect decide what the next step is. It's hard to give up that kind of control, but the fact is you don't have it anyway. Remember that it's the client that writes the check. That's control.

The best forward-moving line I know of is: "Where do you think we should go from here?"

If you and your prospect have remained in rapport through to the end of the call, he will probably want some type of material sent. For only a few products will a prospect want you to visit before he receives something he can feel and read is in his hands and decides you are legitimate.

Once you have agreed to send something, ask another question: "What should we do after that?"

The prospect will invariably tell you he will call you in two weeks. (It's amazing how the majority of people say the exact same thing.) Here's where you have to get a bit assertive, as prospects almost *never* get back to you when they say they will. Use the following dialogue. It works.

> *SDM: So* once I send you the material, what should we do then?
> *Client:* I'll call you in about two weeks.
> *SDM:* Great. I look forward to it on about the 15th. By the way, what happens if you get busy and forget to call? What would you like me to do then?
> *Client:* Well, if I forget to call you, *you call me.*
> *SDM:* Okay. Would you want me to call you on the 16th?
> *Client:* Sure. No, wait. I'm out of town then. Could you call me on the 17th?
> *SDM:* Okay. What time is best?
> *Client:* Mid morning will be fine.
> *SDM:* Should I say anything special to your secretary to let her know you are expecting me to call?
> *Client:* I'll tell her you're calling. Her name is Janet. She'll put you through.
> *SDM:* Thanks a lot. I look forward to speaking to you again. And while you are looking at the material, write down any questions you might have so we can discuss them then. Speak with you soon.

Believe it or not, this conversation will happen about fifteen percent of the time, or following three-quarters of the sales pitches you make. Let's break down how it works.

First, you are offering to put the prospect in the driver seat without attempting to manipulate or control the outcome, although you influence it greatly.

Second, you remain in a "we space," giving your prospect further reasons to trust your intent to serve, rather than sell.

Third, you create an environment of curiosity and anticipation, both for your product or service and for a continuing relationship between you and your client.

And, finally, you are getting an invitation to call back which will, in all likelihood, be honored. (Sometimes the person is not available. In my experience, about twenty-five percent of the time the prospect has left a message for another time to call back. For the other seventy-five percent, you have the secretary's name. You tell her you had an appointment to speak with her boss and ask her what to do. She'll be happy to tell you when to call back. We will discuss the topic of secretaries in Chapter 10, Helpful Hints).

Follow Up Calls

Follow-up calls are essentially the same as cold calls, except you have a lot more rapport and trust built into the conversation. Only after follow-up calls are you in a position to decide with your prospect whether or not you should come out for a visit. You can use the following techniques for following up cold calls or speaking with established customers.

The Introduction

Here are the basic steps to the follow-up introduction:

- Give your name. Get into voice rapport.
- Remind your customer of the reason you are calling and mention something about your last conversation.
- Ask if it's a good time to speak.
- Make some small talk for a brief period of time. Your small talk should be in direct proportion to the amount of time you know the person.

For example:

"Hi, Tom. This is Hal (Jones). If I remember correctly, we were to talk today to discuss the material on Local Area Networks I sent you last week. [This introductory remark will be less formal if you have an established relationship.] Is this a good time for us to speak? You sound a bit less stressed than last time we spoke; (or) You sound busy; (or) Are you well? [And so on.]"

Remember to stay in voice and criterial rapport. If it's a prospect, remember to keep in mind that the two of you need to continue gathering information to be able to decide if you have a basis on which to do business. Be careful about jumping in too soon with ideas or solutions. Since you are still in an introductory phase, keep the customer talking.

• **Ask if the person has had a chance to look at the material you sent.**

Chances are eight out of ten that he has not read the information yet or will not be available to speak with you. I have found that this phase is an important test. The prospect wants to know if you will get pushy, try to sell to him, or be disrespectful in some way. Don't fall into the trap. Maintain the "we space." Say, "Okay. What do you want me to do now?" This maintains the rapport and "we space" and lets the prospect maintain control of the content of the call while you maintain control of the structure.

By the next time you call, this person will have read the information and be ready for the next round of discussions. Remember, you are going for a long-term, growing business relationship, not just a one-time hit. Don't use the phone call as an excuse to make your pitch; you will be wasting your time and an opportunity to further the relationship base. Letting the client decide presupposes trust and wins you points toward establishing a buying environment.

The Primary Sales Pitch

• **If your customer has read your material, get agreement to have a conversation and begin asking questions.**

For example:

"I'm so glad you had a chance to get to it. [Criterial rapport, recognizing the person's busy schedule] Do you have any questions or comments on how you see my product or service working in your environment? [Implicitly getting agreement to begin a conversation.] Could you tell me a bit about how you see us working together? How would my product fit into your environment at this time?"

If the prospect has read your material, there is either a fit or not, but, in either case, there is a shared rapport and understanding around your product. There is certainly enough information on which to base a conversation. And there is interest.

• **Highlight the specific area you will begin discussing.**

Make sure your initial question sets the stage for the conversation. It should be general enough to not get caught in the snag of opening up inappropriate areas of your client's environment, yet specific enough to maintain control of the structure of the conversation. For example:

> "Now that you've read the information, do you think there are areas within your group which could benefit from the maintenance end of my business?" [I'm specifying an area of his business so I can maintain control of the conversation.]

• **Begin to ask questions which will get your customer talking along the lines you wish to pursue.**

By the time you are into a follow-up conversation, you have already built a trust base, so your Inviting questions can be friendlier, and less time spent on Facilitating questions. However, you may spend plenty of time on Organizing questions. (See Organizing Questions on pg. 82.)

At this point, the prospect decides whether to use your product or service or to pass your name on to a colleague. If he decides against buying from you, and you still feel he may not have examined all his alternatives (and you have maintained rapport), you could probably tell him so. Make sure to ask permission first: "Do you mind if I give you another option to consider?" Always give him the option of listening to you or not. At the end of the day, no matter what you believe or what you want, IT'S HIS CALL!

Don't forget to stay in criterial rapport. If you have done so up to this point, and the client is still with you, your chances for a sale or a high-level referral are excellent. Don't blow it by coming in for the kill here. Go back to the original questioning process you used in the cold call, but use the product or service under discussion as your basis. If there is any hint that you are asking self-serving questions, or obviously trying to make a sale, the client will not answer honestly or want to continue the conversation.

The questioning process not only further establishes trust and a "we space," but also uncovers any relevant information your client has stored in less-available indices. (See Chapter 6, Questioning Techniques: Helping A Client Discover Her Needs.) The problem then becomes whether or not he is willing and politically able to deal with these issues now, with you, and with what you are selling.

I was recently trying to get sales training work with a major telecommunications company, and I could not get the prospect to address some of the resource problems he met with daily. We obviously had different maps about what was important. But we had good rapport, and I called him monthly over a long period of time. Finally, after one particularly earnest questioning period, we discovered that a company-wide empowerment training he was running was not giving him the outcome that senior management sorely wanted. Together, we realized the long-term political implications of a less-than-successful program for him. He hired me on the spot to critique the course and rewrite it if necessary. It was decisive, congruent, and quick: he was willing to give me work he'd been unwilling to address himself. While it was not the job I initially wanted to do, it was the job he needed to get done. And, as for me, it was a foot in the door, one which maintained our relationship and enhanced the likelihood of our working together on other projects.

Once rapport is established and the questioning process has begun to delineate your client's environment, he will begin to ask *you* questions, whether or not he is overtly interested in your product at this time. Here is where you should begin your sales pitch.

At this point, whether this is a prospect or an established client, you have gathered enough information to know what this person feels he needs and/or is willing or able to buy.

When What You Have Isn't What They Need
 • **Get a referral when your product is inappropriate but you have achieved a high level of rapport.**

When you are selling only one product or the person is fully covered with your service, and it becomes clear early on that he doesn't need to buy anything from you *according to his map*, the best you can do is get a referral. DO NOT go into a full-fledged sales pitch, as you will break rapport and spoil the possibility for future consideration. Just say:

> "Given that you are telling me you are fully covered and happy with your supplier, it sounds to me like you have no need for my services right now. Do you have any friends or colleagues who aren't covered as well as you and might want to speak with me?"
> (or)
> "It sounds like you have no need for my product right now. Do you have any friends who might need what I have to sell and who you would be willing to refer me to?"

If you have retained rapport throughout, you should get a good referral from the prospect. A personal referral is as good as the rapport you have created with the originator. I have had cold calls turn into business when my phone partner referred me on to a colleague after we had a dynamic and exciting initial call. I make sure to keep in contact with the initial caller and let him know how everything is proceeding. In fact, it sometimes works out that these people become clients months or years later, even though I have never met them. I cannot stress the importance, leverage, and success which good rapport will bring you.

The Close
Eventually, for approximately ten percent of your cold calls and a much higher percent for your established customers, it may become clear that the product or service you are selling is right for this person. It may have taken several more follow-up calls, one or several appointments, or bringing other people into the picture. It may have taken many months, especially for a high-end

item or service sale. But closing a follow-up call continues the process you have followed to this point: it puts the control back in the client's court.

• **Let the prospect tell you how to move the sale forward, once you have agreement.**

For example: "It sounds like you are ready to make a decision. How should we go about this?"

By now, the customer wants to buy. He will have a very clear idea how to proceed. For a service sale, I've had responses like:

• Come and visit the main office to meet the rest of the staff.
• Let's do a series of pilots and go from there.
• Let's start with one course, put all of the "politically correct" people in it, and see if we can get this around the company.
• Send me the person you think we need right now. Once he's settled in, we can add the remaining ones. You can tell me what you think we need after getting input from him.

For a product, you might hear:

• I'm ready to make an order right now. Is there something I need to fill out or can we just do it now?
• Let's try just one of these for now.
• I'd like to see how it works out here, and I'd like to give you a trial on the service end.

Make sure you address each of your client's areas of need and concern by giving specific information or using a story by way of explanation. Additionally, clarify the precise level of service the customer wishes from you, and the time frames in which this service should happen. Regularly sum up what you've heard, and be prepared to implement his requests.

Follow Up After The Sale

When the sale has been completed, make sure you write the customer a letter confirming the entire agreement, from product to service. Call him immediately following the final meeting, sale, or installation, if someone else is doing it. Make sure to check on any problem areas. Let the customer know you two are still in it together. Maintain your "we space." Feel free to call the customer with any thoughts, ideas, problems, or annoyances, and remember the power of the relationship. Just don't take advantage of it. You can be friendly, but not friends.

Once the product or service has been installed or completed, continue to call your client at appropriate intervals; monthly when you provide services, semi-annually when you sell a product. You will continue to get business and referrals from this person as long as you stay in relationship. Even if it has been a one-time sale, you can get plenty of referral business from a happy customer.

Share The "We Space"

I recently was putting on a very expensive training program for a Fortune 500 company. The work took me eight months to bring in, and then we set dates. And set dates again. And again. Since the program was ten consecutive working days, my schedule was ravaged with each change, but, because it was a lucrative job with a new customer, I continued to be flexible. By the fourth time, however, I had had enough. I told the customer I could no longer switch my schedule around, that I'd tried to be respectful of him the other three times, and that now he'd have to be respectful of me. He got the point and we went ahead. It's important to remember that the "we space" works two ways.

When The Prospect Doesn't Return Your Calls

Sometimes you miss the boat, and the customer either was never really interested or lost interest as a result of seeing your material. Too often, this person will not take your follow up calls. If you have not gotten a hold of the person by your third try, leave a message with the secretary. The message should say something to the effect that you have called and are looking forward to touching base in the near future. Clearly state that if he is interested in doing business with you to please return the call. Otherwise, you will keep this person's name on the mailing list and check in with them to say "hi" later in the year. *Not every good phone call will lead to a closed sale. Don't waste your time by chasing people.* I have never heard of a buyer who wanted to buy something but didn't call the supplier! For some reason, we tend to believe that if the person doesn't respond with a buy during one of our calls, he won't call back if he needs us. This is simply not true.

Incoming Calls

Until now, we have dissected outgoing calls. But there are circumstances where our business is about receiving calls and taking orders.

It's obviously much easier to make a sale when a customer calls in to buy or get information about your product. This is the case with the airline industry, car rental companies, the real estate market (to some extent), and with one-of-a-kind products which have few distributors. In this case, the person is already interested and will buy if the information he receives fits in to his criteria, or he has already made a decision to buy and is calling in the order.

When the sale is dependent upon the appropriateness of the information, you already share some criterial rapport and the conversation revolves around the product or service effortlessly. Think about when you are placing an order. Have there been times when you weren't sure you were ready to buy an item before placing the call, but, after having your needs and fears adequately addressed, you placed the order? In the same vein, sales can be lost when you, as the supplier, are out of rapport, or when you don't adequately respond to the questions your client asks. Keep your voice matched through much of the call, and, as well as providing answers, be sure to ask appropriate questions to help the prospect discover anything he is missing.

When the sale is completed, stay in voice rapport (at least in the beginning) and be friendly. I have had instances when I've called to buy something and the attitude of the salesperson has been so task-oriented that I went to another supplier. It's a shame to lose a sale because you lack voice rapport, especially when it is so easy to maintain.

What *Not* To Say And Do

I am in the interesting position of never having been taught what not to say or do. The following techniques work success-fully for me. If they are uncomfortable for you, don't use them. If something you are doing works for you, don't change it. Just know the difference between when it works and when it doesn't.

Do Not Use The Prospect's Name Often

Think about a recent conversation you had with a friend or relative. How many times did you use his name, once past the initial greeting? Probably never, unless you were annoyed. You can have entire conversations with someone you are close with and never mention his name. Using a prospect's name during a sales call is a clear giveaway that it is someone you do not know well. It's a known salesperson's ploy to get the customer to believe in an intimacy which doesn't exist. In fact, NOT using the person's name presupposes relationship.

Skip The Insincere Questions

Do not ask, "How are you today?" when you are making a cold call. People *know* you don't mean it—you are trying to get on their good side to act as if you are friends. But you aren't yet. The question presupposes intimacy before rapport is established. It actually puts you out of rapport.

Don't Impose On The Client's Time

If the person says he only has a few minutes available, don't attempt to start a conversation. You won't be heard or given the time you need and will automatically put yourself out of rapport. Ask for a better time and call back.

Avoid Making A Pitch Unless The Client's Qualified

If a person asks you to talk about your product before you've begun any questioning, don't take the opportunity. It's a trap. This person will use the information against you, much the same way as salespeople have used the information they have gathered for their sales pitch. You are not in a position to discuss your product until and unless your prospect's interests, needs, and criteria have been established.

Don't Oversell
Know how to recognize the signs of an interested prospect. Less is better than more. If you oversell yourself or your product, you will get out of rapport and forfeit trust.

Don't Push A Meeting
Do not tell a customer you are going to be in his area next Thursday at 4:00 and want to drop in. Again, you lose rapport here. When it is time to meet, you will both know it, and it will come about naturally (at the prospect's request).

Delete The Sense Of Urgency
A sale isn't urgent for anyone but the salesperson, in most instances.

Throw Away Methods To Convince, Manipulate, Or Close
Remember, you generally cannot convince anyone to buy anything he doesn't need—at least not more than once. You might as well use the time you are giving this prospect to establish a long-term client who buys regularly.

Don't Talk, Listen
Talk less rather than more. If you remain in rapport and the client wants more information, he will ask you for more. You will know when you are talking too much if you begin to get a voice shift with lots of "uh huhs" and "mms." When that happens, ask the client if you've been talking too much. Give up the control: you've lost it anyway.

Don't Criticize Your Competitors
Do not attempt to put down the competition, especially if the prospect is doing business with them. By doing so, you are putting down the prospect's decision making.

Don't Leave Your Name

Don't leave your name with a secretary if you haven't gotten into rapport with her, as she will not make a compelling case for her boss to return your call. Also, you will be waiting to hear from him without knowing if he has decided not to call, didn't have time to call, or didn't get your message. If you place another call when he doesn't return yours, you are out of rapport and at a disadvantage. You have a chance only if the secretary will tell the boss to expect your call at a prearranged time she has given you or if you keep calling until you reach him. (See Chapter 10, Helpful Hints.)

Don't Linger

Be friendly, not friends. Monitor the amount of time you spend on each call. Except in rare instances, no call should be more than seven minutes. If you are not able to complete most calls in which you are actually making a pitch in less than seven minutes, you are giving too much information on a first call or using too much time to get into rapport. *Long calls keep you involved with people who like to talk, not buy.* Even people with whom you have instant rapport are busy. So are you. Get on to the next call.

With the budget and environment to do so, I don't know of any client who will not buy a needed product from a person he trusts. Trust the customer will buy. You don't have to sell.

Skill Set 9

How to listen

1. Begin to notice the flow of your current conversations. Either tape record a conversation or jot down notes afterwards. Notice who speaks, when, and how often. Notice at what point in the conversation you begin your pitch. Are you using the prospect's buying patterns? Are you addressing the stated or discovered needs, or selling according to your own needs?
2. Begin to keep track of your pitch. Is it the same for everyone? How do you alter it? When and for whom? Do you use different types of pitches? Under which conditions do they change?
3. Do you have a way of knowing if you are being successful? Unsuccessful? Make a picture in your mind's eye of a successful cold call and an unsuccessful one. What are the differences in the pictures? How are you sitting? What words do you use? Notice the difference in the way you use your voice and words. Do you use stories in either? Make sure to note the differences between what you say and how you say it in a call that eventually leads to a sale and one that doesn't.
4. What percentage of your cold or referral calls currently result in full-fledged pitches? What percentage do you close? What percentage of your face-to-face appointments result in sales? Is there a pattern to the wasted ones (many no-shows; prospects inadequately qualified because of money, timing, benefits, and so on)?
5. Note the differences in your voice and language patterns between cold calls, follow-up calls, and referral calls. Is there anything which isn't working or you would like to change?

6. Break down the new, recommended conversation techniques in this chapter into your introduction, pitch, and close. Practice one a day for three days. Then, on the fourth and fifth days, use at least parts of all three. Take notes on your progress, what works, what doesn't, and how. Try practicing one a day again the next week. Continue until you have integrated those parts of the techniques which work for you.

7. Break down your follow-up calls. Is there anything you would like to add or subtract? How do you currently create an opportunity for your prospects to discuss the material you sent them?

8. Note your closing strategy. Again, listen to a tape recording of your close if possible. Do you always ask for an appointment? Do you believe it is possible to make a sale without asking for an appointment until your prospect is appropriately qualified by phone? Do you believe that every person is a potential client? Do you attempt to convince in your pitch? Are you willing to give up trying to maintain control?

9. Do you use a script? What are the components of the script you currently find beneficial? Problematic? Which parts would you like to keep? Throw away? Are you willing to work without a script? If not, what could you add to what you are currently doing that would enhance your approach?

Helpful Hints

Now that we know how to get into rapport, disassociate, listen, question, make cold calls, follow-up, qualify, and close, let's examine to some of the specific situations you may face.

Qualifying A Prospect

There is no reason you must visit people in order to qualify them. You can get all the information you need to create the rapport and gather the needed information from each client over the phone—and visit only those prospects who are qualified and who want to meet with you.

For Prospects Using Your Competitor's Product Or Service

It is often easier to sell a product when a need has already been established than to go through the process of discovering the need. When the prospect is using your competitor's product or service, this will come out in the first few seconds of the call. However, once she answers you in any way whatsoever, *so long as she doesn't hang up,* you have the beginnings of a "we space." Even if the person *says* she has enough, or doesn't want any, *she is still talking to you and wants something from the call, or she would hang up!* I get real curious about a prospect who tells me she is content using my product or service through a different supplier, but is willing to talk to me anyway. She is speaking with me out of some type of need she is not initially expressing: inadequate service, insufficient product, discomfort with current price structures, curiosity about alternate price structures, or possible future resource needs.

After the normal cold call opening, start asking Facilitating questions to find out about the environment in which your type of product or service is being used. Your client's response to this first set of questions will tell you a lot about the appropriateness of continuing the conversation. You might be very curious— which product specifically? How is it being used? How is it being accepted? What are the contents of the course? Is she happy with the product? Make sure you stay in voice rapport here, as it won't take much for the prospect to lose trust (or not have it at all) in regard to your curiosity. Remember that your job is to set up an environment, not to make a pitch.

There are many people who are very comfortable using the product and want no additional support—regardless of whether you believe they are in need. I once spoke with a training manager who put all 700 of his people through a twelve-week (twelve weeks!) customer service program which taught them how to perform tasks around customer care. (Answer a call or letter within X amount of time; the customer is always right, and so on.) No one taught them how to get into rapport or how to see a problem from a customer's standpoint. I felt a twelve-week program on picking up the phone by the third ring, or having appropriate information handy on your newly organized desk, did not deal fully with the problem. But when I remarked that it was obvious to me that the program was a success for him, "I am SO happy I cannot tell you. We have been getting the highest marks on the industry-standard surveys for customer satisfaction, and that's as good as it gets in my book." I told him I was really happy for him, that obviously we needn't waste our time talking about my program. I said, "I guess there's always room for improvement, but in this case I agree with you." But I asked if he could give me a referral to a group in his company that was not so successful as he was and didn't have the time or the funds for a twelve-week program. He did this happily, as well as ask to be put on our mailing list. Through this conversation, I gained an interested prospect for mailing list and a referral. (By the way, the reason the man spoke to me was to brag about his success. And I was happy to let him.)

Facilitating and/or Specifying questions will bring out any problems for people who are using your product or service but are unhappy with how it is maintaining itself or how the supplier is supporting them. It is imperative that you do not ask directly about their problems with the supplier, as it will create a defensive position and diminish your ability to gain trust. As discussed in Chapter 6, Questioning Techniques, when a prospect says she is happy, I usually tell her that it sounds like she is doing well and has it all under control. This will give her room to examine any possible inadequacies independently.

For Prospects *Not* Using Your Product Or Service

These prospects fall into three categories:

- those who are not using my product because they don't need it
- those who need it but don't know that they do
- those who know they need it but haven't purchased it due to environmental, political, or monetary factors.

The first is easiest. There are some people who just don't need your product or service. I know many sales people believe that if they are convincing enough, anyone is a potential buyer. I don't believe that, and I believe this attitude is disrespectful of the client. I *do* believe, however, that every call can at least get you a referral so long as you stay in rapport.

When a prospect is not using your product or service because she is unaware of the need, the questioning techniques outlined in Chapter 6 will assist her in discovering the areas which need attention, should there be any. As we discussed earlier, a client is often locked into her present situation, and she has yet to discover a possible discrepancy between her present state and her desired one. Again, through rapport (lots of rapport!) and questions, a prospect can become your client if there is a real need. I will say again that it is *not your job* to "create" a need, only to *facilitate in the discovery of one.*

Your job is one of an investigator to find out:

- the specific reasons why she has not bought before this
- what specific conditions your prospect requires to be ready to buy
- what has stopped her from making long-range plans with another salesperson
- if it is possible to set up the sales in pieces or segments so the time frame or budget will not be so adversely affected
- if this person would be willing to continue a long-term dialogue with you with the intent of purchasing from you when the time is right
- if it is appropriate to get the prospect to see you or your product now to have an idea of what is available.

Remember to tread carefully here. The prospect doesn't want to be rushed, and your map will clearly be different than hers in terms of a time frame. I had two instances with major telecommunications companies who had budgetary problems but were in need of training. I called them regularly, even in their cars. I kept rapport going over many months. I had numerous dead-ended meetings, promises, and rejections, but the contacts were good and the rapport was wonderful. Finally, after six months in one case and thirteen months in another, the jobs and budgets came through. They were lucrative, fun contracts which kept me busy and the customer happy. The trick was to hang in without hanging on, and use the time to build a level of trust that allowed me the flexibility to create what I believed needed to be done, once I began the work.

For Prospects Who Are Constantly Solicited By Phone
If you supply a standard service or product, such as stocks, insurance, and so on, it is an exercise in futility to attempt to convince a prospect that your service or product is different from

the rest. What is the difference between one company's Whole Life insurance policy and another's? Or between a specific laser printer from one store or another? Talk about what the customer wants, and what you have to sell: relationship. An ad in our local newspaper exhibited this point. It was for a Mercedes Benz dealership, with no discussion of the specific cars available, or what was special about a Mercedes. In fact, there was nothing in the ad about the car itself. Everyone knows what a Mercedes is, does, and represents. Either you want one or you don't. The ad was about quality service and customer support: "If you want to buy the car, then buy it from us!" They were selling their dealership, not the car.

Unless you have a well-defined product which is different than any in the marketplace, what sets you apart is the relationship you build with your customer. I was able to open 210 new accounts my first six months as a stockbroker because people liked spending time with me on the phone. I didn't have financial expertise. I didn't have experience. But I liked them, and they could tell.

When calling to qualify a prospective client who gets solicited constantly, instant rapport is vital. These people really do not want to be bothered again. Criterial rapport is just as important here as voice rapport. Let the person know you know he doesn't want to be solicited.

> "Hi. My name is Phillip Durant and I assist people with their insurance needs. You must get lots of these calls, huh?"
> (or)
> "Hello. My name is Phillip Durant and I work with people's insurance needs when they have them. Are you covered in all the ways you want to be covered?"

Notice the use of Closed questions in both instances. If they answer and don't hang up, the conversation will continue. This offers the beginnings of a "we space." Occasionally, these people will hang up, but many would anyway when they hear an insurance person on the line, regardless of the way the call is approached. But in each instance, they are *not* being given a pitch and you are attempting to get them to feel comfortable (as in the first example), or you are getting them to ask themselves questions about their existing coverage right away. In either instance, there is a chance they will speak with you if they trust they are not being coerced into buying. That brings up another opening approach:

> "My name is Phillip Durant. I'm in the insurance industry, but I really have nothing to sell you if you don't need to buy anything. Are you fully covered?"

No matter how often these people have been solicited, people rarely hang up on you if you have gotten into voice and/or criterial rapport with them.

After the prospect responds to the Closed question by saying she is fully covered or in some way doesn't need your product or service, it's your turn to speak. You then affirm her coverage:

> "That's great. I rarely get to speak with someone who is FULLY COVERED."

It is now the prospect's turn to speak.

One of two things will happen here. Either she will continue to affirm she has no needs (which may be true) or start to back down. If she continues to state she has no needs, ask for a referral.

If she is still speaking with you, and has nothing to buy from you, the conversation is continuing because she likes you. A referral might be in order:

> "It sounds like you have all your needs covered. I'm glad for you. Do you know anyone you'd be willing to refer to me about possible needs? I realize people have insurance from the time they're young, but sometimes they need to add more coverage. Would you feel comfortable giving me a name?"

By this time, you are in rapport and the prospect believes you are not trying to sell something she doesn't want. She will either reassess her own program or pass on a name. Make sure to ask if she'd like to receive one of your cards in case of future needs. The worst that will happen is that she'll take your card and never use it. Sometimes she'll call you months later. And sometimes she will say "no." Chances are great you will get something from this call if they have followed it through this far.

Occasionally, when you ask someone if she has all her needs met, she will say "no." At this point, you want to go into your Facilitating, Specifying, and Organizing questions, just as you would in any other information-gathering call. You can qualify the person and save yourself and your prospect the time of a wasted visit.

Don't offer too much information during the first call. End the call by letting the prospect decide where to go from here. You can both decide during the second call if a face-to-face is appropriate. And remember that if the prospect is obviously avoiding your second call, put the name in the dead file and don't waste any more time.

Working *With* Secretaries

The question I am most often asked is, "How do you get past the secretary?" The answer is, you don't. Every person you contact on the phone is a potential relationship. Therefore, you work *with* the secretary, not *past* her.

When I was a stockbroker in the late '70s, we had specific work areas for four-person teams. Each day at lunchtime, one person stayed behind to cover the phones for the other three. One day, when it was my turn to cover, a phone began ringing incessantly. I picked it up and the conversation went like this:

"Hello! I want some service here!
"Yes sir! How can I help you?"
"I want to place an order. I want a broker!"
"Yes sir! What can I do for you?"
"DID YOU HEAR ME? I SAID I WANT A BROKER!"
"Yes sir. I heard you. I'm here and I'm ready to take your order."

> *"IS THERE SOMETHING WRONG WITH YOU? I WANT*
> *A BROKER!"*
> "I'm a broker, sir."
> "You are? Oh . . .Um . . .Would you please take an order
> for me?"

I was shaking when I got off the phone. I couldn't imagine why anyone would speak like that to a stranger. It took me days to realize that that was the way many men spoke to secretaries in those days, and, because he wasn't used to a female broker, he assumed I was a secretary. From what I understand, although this was a severe case, men still treat secretaries as if they aren't people. When I have given this example in my courses, I have heard many secretaries mumble that it sounded too familiar.

Therefore, when they get a chance to exert some control, they do. And, let's be honest, who's got the control? You or the secretary?

A secretary can be my best ally. I once got into such good rapport with a woman during a cold call that she went into the men's room to get her boss to come and speak with me.

To get into rapport with a secretary, I follow all of the same rules as on a cold- or follow-up call. I use my voice to get into rapport and get into criterial rapport as soon as possible. I even make my voice a bit softer to let her know that I know she's in control. I trust that she will make sure I get to speak with the person I should be speaking with (which may not, in fact, be the person I'm trying to get a hold of). After all, it's her job to assist her boss. Let me give you some examples of typical cold call greetings:

> "Hello. My name is Sharon Drew Morgen. I'm wonder-
> ing if you can help me. I am a communications skills
> consultant and I'm wondering if your company has any
> training or needs for training in communication skills."

After using this opening with the secretary of the regional vice president at a major computer company, she said, "Hang on a minute." She left me on hold for three minutes, came back, and said, "Are you in town next Tuesday morning at 8:00? The assistant to the VP is just coming back from vacation and will want to see you. I've set up an appointment for him to see you first thing." Note that in the above example, I did *not* ask for her boss. I treated her as the person who could help me—and she did. Another greeting is:

> "Hello. My name is Sharon Drew Morgen. I don't know if you are the right person I should be speaking with, but maybe if I tell you what I'm calling about, you might be able to tell me what to do."

This approach works well, as it gets right into the highly valued criterion of assisting others in getting a job done well. It always gets me put through to the person I need to be speaking with.

My favorite example happened while I was training someone one-to-one. Her conversation with a secretary went like this:

Secretary: Hello. This is Brenda. May I help you?
Client: Yes. I'd like to speak with Mary Nelson, please.
Secretary: I'm sorry. Ms. Nelson is not in. May I take a message?

After my client left her name and hung up, she went to make the next call and I stopped her. "What happened there?" I asked. She responded: "What do you mean? It was just a normal call. Mary wasn't in." I asked for the number and dialed it myself. By focusing on building relationship instead of performing a task, the results were amazing.

Secretary: Hello. This is Brenda. May I help you?
SDM: Hi, Brenda. This is Sharon!
Secretary: Hi, Sharon. Do I know you?
SDM: No. Do I know you?
Secretary: (Laughter.) I don't think so. Can I help you?
SDM: I'm trying to get a hold of Mary Nelson, and I know she's real busy and not in much. Is this one of those times?

Secretary: Yes, but she's working out of her house today and I can give you the number.

I got into voice rapport, got into relationship with her immediately by matching her name usage, and matched her criteria around having a boss who was always out of the office. I assumed she was free to give out Mary's number to whomever she thought should have it. And I knew her boss about as well as my client did—not at all. Matching is powerful business. (A word of caution here: don't use the secretary's name just to use it. You will come off as being insincere, as it assumes an intimacy you don't have. Only use the name if it is given to you with the "hello," or ask for it at the end of the conversation if she has been helpful and you wish to personally thank her, or you will have continued contact.)

Here are two other simple examples:

"Hello. My name is Sharon Drew Morgen. I'm making a sales call to your company and don't even know the right person to speak to. If I explain to you what I'm selling, would you tell me what you think I should do?"
(or)
"Hello. This is Sharon Drew Morgen. Are you Mr. Jones' assistant?"

Remember that a secretary has inside knowledge which you don't have. She's got the connections, the control, and the authority. She's the keeper of the gate. Be respectful of her.

Think for a minute of ways you have tried to get past the secretary by using a forceful voice and knowing the prospect's name. If the secretary feels like it, you can get through. But it's random. Try getting into rapport and give yourself some choices. Secretaries will give you any information you need: names of department heads, deadlines, budget dates, influential people. There's a new word around the business world these days: *coach*, or someone on the inside who can help you. Let the secretary be your coach.

What To Do With Voice Mail

People don't seem to know what to do with voice mail. For me, there are two rules. If you are trying to speak with someone who she is not expecting your call, DON'T LEAVE ANY MESSAGE unless you have tried every other way to get to contact her (like calling her secretary and throwing yourself on her mercy to give you a specific time to call). If you know this is the correct person to be speaking with, and you have called countless times, leave a message. In some ways voice mail is good: you get the ear of your prospect for as long as you want it and get to throw a free pitch to an otherwise unattainable person. Just use the following guidelines.

Listen carefully to the message. Match the voice tone, tempo, and pitch as exactly as possible. Speak as if you were having a whole (but one-sided) conversation:

> "Hi. This is Joseph Penta. You don't know me, and this is a cold call, so I guess I'm going to have to talk to myself because I've tried to reach you and have not had any luck. I don't even know if you want to talk, or if it would be beneficial for you to speak to me, but I can tell you a bit about what I wanted to speak to you about now. I sell insurance, but I'm not the typical kind of insurance broker because I specialize in customer service. I really have nothing to sell you unless you have needs . . . "

Go for it. You have nothing to lose. If you show yourself to be a relationship-oriented person and you have matched her voice and criteria around being busy, you have a foot in the door. There's a fifty-fifty chance she'll call back if you use this approach.

Referrals

You can ask for a referral after *any* conversation. If you are in rapport with the prospect and have gotten into a "we space," they will reject only the need for your product or service, not you.

They are often willing to give you a referral even after a brief chat.

When you call people to whom you have been referred, it's appropriate to throw in a bit of small talk about the person who referred you prior to launching in to the questioning process. For example:

> *SDM:* Hello. This is Sharon Drew Morgen and I am in the insurance industry. I was given your name by Paula Smith as she thought there was a possibility you may want to take a look at some of your insurance needs.
>
> *Prospect:* I hadn't really thought about it. Do you know Paula well?
>
> *SDM:* No. I just called her on a cold call and we had a lovely conversation. She was comfortable with her coverage for now. She seems like a lot of fun. Have you known her long?
>
> *Prospect:* Yes. And she really is lots of fun. But I don't have any needs either.
>
> *SDM:* Would you know of someone who might be reexamining their portfolio or be willing to give me another referral?

Don't ever lie and tell the prospect you know the referral better than you do, because she'll find out in seconds.

Using the name of a prospect's friend is a quick way to get into rapport. If the person is willing to discuss possible needs with you, follow the same format as cold calls: use the questions to help the prospect discover her potential needs.

Ongoing Client Contact

Discussions with long-standing clients have a great deal of flexibility up front. Small-talk, catch-up conversations, and open-ended discussions may take place since voice and criterial rapport have already been established.

There are myriads of reasons to have regular phone contact with your ongoing clientele. We will look at those used most often. Don't forget that the outcome of all calls remains the same—the establishment of an environment in which clients can get their needs met.

Customer Service

Part of every business is ongoing service. Many salespeople believe that their sale is a one-time deal once the product is paid for. However, if you believe that a customer is a long-term relationship, you will maintain contact and reap the benefits of follow-up business and referrals. I have also had many instances where a customer has moved to a different company and has brought me and my services along with her.

Before, during, and after every job or installation or sales, I call the customer to check that everything is as it should be. Is everything in place? Working as expected? Did the delivery go according to plan? Is the product operating properly? Did the participants like the course? The trainers? Is there anything else needed from me at this point? For the future? Of course, if you are taking phone orders for a product which is sent to hundreds of people a day, this level of contact is unnecessary. But if there is a large order involved, call.

"Hello Calls"

I also call my clients regularly, as I would my long-distance friends, to maintain the relationship. I call these calls "Hello Calls." They have no purpose other than relationship mainte-nance—because the client matters to me. On these calls, I keep the conversation light and about non-business related topics. If there was a selling opportunity, I might address it by sending a short note, calling back the next day, or even calling back directly after hanging up if she really wants to address a business issue. ("Hi Susan. It's me again. This is a sales call.") In this way, customers look forward to my call as being part of our relationship, not a way for me to sneak in a spiel.

Initially, before clients understand what I'm doing on these calls, they want to get into business problems, but I tell them I really just called to say "hi" and wanted to find out about their vacation, or share with them a funny thing that happened to me.

I place these calls once a month for large clients, and every two or three months for smaller ones. When clients get used to hearing from me regularly with my "Hello Calls," they miss them when I don't make them. I've had clients call, asking, "Where's my 'Hello Call' this month?" It's amazing the results this contact brings. I am always the first supplier thought of when new business comes in; I get called immediately without rancor whenever there's a problem, just to request my assistance; referrals come in regularly; and I have a friend. By taking the time to make this type of contact, you will only have to find a small percentage of new clients annually, instead of playing catch-up by replacing lost business.

And who do I consider my "clients" who should be called? Not just my paying customers, but my staff and my own suppliers. In my computer company, I called the technical contractors in the field (as well as my full-time staff, of course) on a monthly basis. The company which supplied the fourth generation computer language we supported used to call me after installing the product, saying, "We just got the software in! How do you have people in here already?"

Because I was in constant contact with the field, I heard all the gossip on the grapevine: who was moving, who was having trouble, what areas were doing what. Naturally, I acted on this information. But I wouldn't have been able to be proactive without the loyalty of my field staff. And I gained their loyalty by making sure I had regular contact.

Service Calls

I also make regular calls to customers I supply with an on-going service, to make sure all is going well. This usually catches problems at an early stage. I also elicit constant feedback from field personnel when appropriate. Sometimes peripheral people are causing problems and need a phone call or a visit. My staff used to joke that the longest anyone (client or staff) got away with anything that I didn't hear about was six hours. I had such a vast network of loyal people as a result of my continual contact that I was called as soon as a problem began emerging.

Supporting Errors

I believe that customer service is the root of all business. After all, without customers there is no business. Too often, companies put their task first and forget the relationship. Many companies make their customer bear the brunt of their errors. A large industrial company I worked with often has difficulty delivering their product on time. Instead of working with the customer to help with the problems caused by delays, they just call, give the new date, and end the conversation. Let me give you an example:

Supplier: Hi, Joe. This is Don. I have some bad news for you.

Client: Again?

Supplier: Well, we're going to have to change that date again because there was a mix up in orders and they didn't finish production on your order. They've promised me they'd have it out early next week.

Client: That's not good enough.

Supplier: Well, there's nothing we can do about it. I'll try to make sure that next time it works out.

Client: I'll believe it when I see it.

In this example, which I listened into during a consultancy project, the customer gets no relief from the effects of the supplier's error. That behavior is the reason this company has been losing revenue and staff for years. Here's the way a similar conversation went when they learned to have contact from a relationship base:

Supplier: Hi, Glen. This is Barbara. I have some bad news for you that you're not going to like a lot and which doesn't please me either. Are you ready?

Client: Are you going to change my delivery date again?

Supplier: Yes.

Client: Damn it. That puts off my whole schedule.

Supplier: I'm sure it does. I wish I could tell you we could get it to you before next week but we can't. Tell me what that does to your schedule.

Client: I have a team ready tomorrow to start our new

project. I have nothing else to do with them. I'll have to
pay them anyway. And that means the product will be
late for our customers.
Supplier: That stinks. Will it help if I send letters to your
customers apologizing for the delay so you don't have to
bear the brunt of it?
Client: Yes, actually, that will help.
Supplier: How about any compensation we can offer to
help defray the costs of the down time?
Client: Sounds great, but there's no way we can handle the
accounting on that.
Supplier: Well, how about if I give you a better price on the
order. Will that help?
Client: It'll help calm my boss down. I really appreciate
your taking the time to do this for us. I wish we didn't
have the problem in the first place, but I realize it happens. Thanks for your concern.

The first conversation led to the customer filing a complaint
by contacting higher management. He also might have found a
new supplier. The second conversation maintained the relationship, offered support, and took the heat off of the problem. It
takes a few extra minutes in the short term, but saves time and
revenue in the long term.

That kind of caring can also operate in the professional
service industry. Take dentistry. Recently, I had a bad cavity
which I had filled. Over the weekend, I got a toothache ten times
worse than the original one. My gums swelled and the pain went
into my ears. I spent part of Saturday night looking for homeo-
pathic remedies to kill the pain, as I had no prescription from the
dentist, who did not respond to the messages I left on his
machine. On Monday morning, I went back and was told he
didn't have time to see me until the next day. Needless to say, by
the time I finished my end of the conversation, the receptionist
put me ahead of the next patient. Following additional work, I
went home only to have the pain start again. This time I went to
a new dentist who took an X-ray and found that the work the first
dentist had done had gone into my tooth's root and caused an

infection. He began a root canal right away. By Saturday, I had an abscess and a fever. I called the second dentist. He was kind enough to call me back and get me a prescription. But the prescription didn't help, and I was in agonizing pain the rest of the weekend. When I went in to the office Monday morning and told him of the pain, he said that if I'd have called a second time, which he'd kind of expected, he would have come into the office on an emergency basis. I was stunned. I asked him, "Why didn't you call me back and find out how I was doing?" Now it was his turn. "You're right. I never thought of it."

Don't forget people. Any problems inherent in your task can be overcome through relationship.

Incoming Calls

Most of our discussions have been around outgoing calls where *we* want something from the person we are speaking with. There are occasions and work situations, however, when incoming calls are the issue. Clients and new customers call in to place orders, lodge complaints, gather information, ask questions, and request referrals for additional suppliers.

Always create and maintain rapport by first getting into voice rapport by matching her "hello." Depending on how well you know your phone partner and how much criterial rapport you have established with her, use matching strategies as best you can to ask how you can help. For any incoming call (I'll speak on complaint calls separately), asking Facilitating and lots of Summary questions works best. For example:

- "Let me make sure I understand you. Are you saying . . . ?"
- "I'm going to repeat what you just said . . . Is that right?"
- "Would you mind if I repeat all that? Please stop me if I've got any of this wrong."
- "Let me repeat the requirements as you stated them . . . "

Since an incoming caller wants something very specific, you must make certain she gets what she wants. At the end of the conversation, ask if she has gotten what she needs, or if she still has some questions which weren't asked. AT&T has a wonderful question at the end of their customer service conversations:

"Did you get the service you needed? Were you happy with the service you received?"

Tread lightly with incoming calls. After all, people who call in are interested in your product or service, or already using it. Since they are the ones who want something from the call, it is their responsibility to get what they need from it. In this case, sit back, get into rapport (voice and criterial) and do not be aggressive. Be polite, helpful, and informed. Be patient. With rapport and the right questions, you will get your order.

Complaints

Complaints require some judgment on your part. When a caller is annoyed, she is associated, out of rapport, and happy to remain so. I assume, however, that there is a desire on the part of the complainer to reach a solution or at least some type of agreement. Otherwise, she would not have called, but done something like called the big boss, the Attorney General, or your licensing association, or would have sent the product back or refused to pay for the service. The fact that this person called shows willingness to find a solution and to remain in relationship with you and your company.

There are two ways to go, depending on how well you know the complainant. You can match her voice or you can mismatch it.

By **matching** the caller's loud, annoyed voice (but not her angry words), you will get into voice rapport and make her comfortable. I know you have always been trained to be soft and gentle when a customer calls, especially when she is angry. But remember a time when you had an argument with your spouse and s/he was loud and furious. What happened when you stayed calm? S/he went ballistic, right? This is because you were out of rapport. Believe it or not, if you can move toward matching the tone, tempo, and volume of an angry person, you will calm her down. It will become apparent to her that you care, because she will unconsciously realize you are both coming from the same place. It may go against your inclinations. Initially say something like, *"I hear you are annoyed, Mr. Jones!"* Just try it. Keep moving the volume down a notch until both of you are using a quieter tone.

Mismatching an angry customer's voice will work more often if you already know the person and you have a history of conversations. By being gentle, soft, and helpful, you might calm down the caller, but you might also make her angrier. Try out both methods. Occasionally, when you use this gentle voice, your customer will immediately disassociate, be aware of the disparity, feel out of rapport, and calm down. If this doesn't work, try matching her voice instead.

As to questions, use a number of Summary questions. Keep repeating what she said, and ask her if you got it right. This will serve two functions: to ensure you get all of the information, and to let the caller know you remain interested in helping her. This behavior alone, if nothing else is done about her problem, will go a long way toward helping her feel better. Once you understand the problem, ask your phone partner what she would like done. Of course, you may not be able to provide the specific solution, but if you hear the expectation, you know where you stand. It's easier to deal with the realities of the expectation than to spend time exploring the realities of what you can and cannot offer, (which forces you to face your client's rebuffs and annoyance). Both of you will feel frustrated.

The better you can maintain a "we space," the more latitude the complainant will give you in terms of time and solutions. An incoming complaint call is one area where it is appropriate for you, not your client, to accept responsibility for uncovering a solution.

I once had a problem with my brokerage house. (In this instance, I was the client with a complaint.) There was an outstanding check I received from a foreign bank which was not finding its way into my account. I knew from my customer who wrote the check that it had cleared weeks prior. It was a relatively large check, and I needed the funds as soon as possible. I called my broker, who either wouldn't take my calls or told me he could do nothing to help me since he couldn't contact the Foreign desk. He kept saying that the check would find its way and not to worry about it. He completely mismatched my criterion. I needed him to find a solution. I finally got so annoyed that I called his boss, who sweetly told me she'd make some calls and find out what happened. She kept in contact with me, and I went through the searching process with her. When she didn't return one of my calls, I got annoyed with her and she got annoyed right back, telling me she was doing the best she could for me but that several departments were involved and not all of them were on my time schedule. This calmed me down, as I realized that she had been supportive and responsive for the three prior days, and I was not the only person needing assistance from this woman. We got back to business. After two more days, the check was found. I appreciated her work and wrote her a thank you note. And I dropped my broker.

With rapport and trust, even difficult situations can be handled easily. Had the broker later called and apologized for his lack of concern, I would have accepted his apology and we would have continued. But the problem was swept under the carpet, making me feel like I didn't count. And why should I choose to be serviced by someone who doesn't care about me?

Continually asking questions about what the complainant needs, maintaining rapport, matching criteria around the desired outcome, regularly using summary questions, returning phone calls (or having your staff return them to say you cannot get back to them at that moment) will let the caller know you want to offer as much assistance as possible to meet her needs. It's not about who's right; it's about relationship and respect. I have found that how we respond to problems either makes or breaks business relationships. Problems provide an opportunity to cement your reliability and trustworthiness and to prove your desire to provide service.

Skill Set 10

Helpful hints

1. Categorize your current qualifying calls. How many are with prospects who already use your product or service? With people who don't? How do you find out? What strategies are you currently using to uncover unaddressed needs?
2. When qualifying a prospect, begin using questioning techniques to gather the appropriate information and facilitate the process of getting from the present situation to the desired one. Begin to notice the difference between people who have an obvious need and those whose needs are less obvious and require more questioning from you. What do you need to do to facilitate this person's discovery process?
3. Do you have an easier time getting into rapport with some prospects than with others? Break down the differences. Identify any patterns so you can have choice for new behaviors when it's difficult to build rapport.
4. Do you currently behave or speak differently with people you instinctively like or dislike (matched or mismatched maps)? What are the differences? What, specifically, do you need to do to give yourself flexibility on any call?
5. How do you currently approach secretaries? Begin to work with them through a relationship filter and note the differences in the responses you get.

6. Do you ask for referrals regularly? If not, what stops you? Try it for a week and note the results.

7. Do you currently make regular contact with existing clientele? Set aside a day to call your regular or larger customers. Again, note the results. Try "Hello Calls" for a month. Make sure you include suppliers and support staff.

8. Are there any areas of client contact in which you historically put task first?

9. How do you currently handle problem or complaint calls? What new techniques can you use when what you are doing isn't working so well?

Time Management And The Phone

Chapter

11

Unless you are in the telemarketing business, the telephone will be only one of the business tools you use. The day gets filled with meetings, paperwork, and projects with time commitments. With a well-planned week and structured day, you can fit in everything that you need to do and still place a minimum of forty, if not sixty, calls a day.

Breaking Down The Day

Workdays have a definite structure. People arrive, settle in, work, have a break, work, take lunch, settle in, work, have a break, work, get ready to leave, and leave. The time frame of each is dependent upon the job description. Junior people generally arrive later, leave earlier, and have longer breaks. Senior people arrive earlier, stay later, and break infrequently, except for the occasional business lunch. With those parameters in mind, calling time becomes easy: The more senior the person, the earlier or later you call, so as not to conflict with meetings.

A day devoted to phone contact might look something like this:

8:00-8:15	Arrive and settle in
8:15-9:15	Cold call senior prospects
9:15-9:30	Break
9:30-11:00	Call managers and existing clients
11:00-11:15	Break: check incoming messages, mail; say "hi" to secretary, colleagues, staff
11:15-Noon	Return calls, speak with suppliers
Noon-2:00	Lunch break, paperwork, notetaking, thinking, and informal meetings
2:00-3:30	Call support people, existing clients
3:30-5:45	Cold call senior prospects and break
5:45-6:30	Record keep, organize follow-up

Your day is being used to maximize the normal flow. When people are around, you are on the phone. When people are on breaks, you are doing work which does not involve speaking. Call when they're there, don't call when they're not.

Going After New Business

Fifty percent of your phone time should be spent getting new business, whether by referral or cold calling. This will ensure a continued flow of new business coming in. My first few months in my fledgling computer company were spent cold calling. When people began responding, I spent the next month visiting, doing paperwork, writing contracts, and hiring. Once that was completed, and my first clients were in place and getting appropriate support, I found that there was no new business coming in. I had forgotten to continue calling for ongoing business. I had to start all over again with another two month gap with no new business.

New-business calls should be made at least three days per week, and two one-and-one-half-hour segments per day is minimal. When I cold call, I make fifty cold calls to brand new people each calling day. Of these, I expect to reach approximately twenty people, although it varies. The trick is to KEEP GOING. I do not use this calling time to take notes or make up information booklets; I do all that after my calling hours, either during the lunch break or after hours. I also do not take incoming calls. In most industries, people are understanding around a call-back an hour later.

Breaking Down The Numbers

You might think that fifty calls per day is difficult, if not impossible, to achieve. It would be difficult for me to achieve that number also if I made pitches to all the people I contacted. Again, I only pitch to approximately twenty percent of the people I reach (ten out of the fifty, or five out of twenty-five), since the rest are not qualified. Out of twenty-five contacts, I will spend no more than five minutes each with twenty of them (an average of one-and-one-half-hours total calling time) and ten minutes with each of the other five. Add to that the time it takes placing calls to the other twenty who are not reachable (say, one minute each), maybe a short stretch break in the middle, and you have a total of three hours to place fifty cold calls, make twenty-five contacts, and give five pitches to five qualified prospects. Do this three times a week, and you will have fifteen qualified prospects a week, about sixty-five per month. That will potentially bring in thirty new clients per month! Not to mention what the calls to existing clients, suppliers, and field staff will bring in.

One of the best ways of getting new business is from existing, satisfied customers. Set aside at least one hour on each call-day for service calls, bringing your total call time to approximately four hours per call day. Check in with existing customers—either those you haven't seen or spoken with in a few weeks, those just beginning to use your services or product, or those who have been having a problem. (As discussed in Chapter 10, Helpful Hints, customers, no matter how small, should be contacted regularly to maintain a relationship.) Your call will tell them you care, you are with them, and they can trust you. These people will have no doubt as to whom to refer their friends or whom to call again for add-on business.

Here is a helpful hint for your cold calling periods. When I make a series of calls in which I face rejection, although my prospects are always respectful, I need a booster to keep me going for the next round. I then call a favorite supplier or a funny customer. It's a perfect opportunity to touch base and maintain relationship, and it gives me a picker-upper.

A Note On "Urgency"

For some reason, salespeople seem to think that sales have an urgent time frame. When a customer has a need he wants only you and your company to fill, there is no other competitor who will take the business away. It's yours. You can call back in an hour, or the next day. Of course, if there is a problem, it must be handled urgently, and make sure your secretary or voice mail is set up to respond to problems. I'm always amazed that when I tell people to make only outgoing calls during their calling time, they panic and wonder what will happen if they are unavailable when a prospect calls to place an order. That person will wait for you to call back. He will most probably not call the next available supplier if rapport, trust, and a "we space" have been set up between you.

If you set aside three days a week with the preceding schedule, the other two days can be spent in the field or in meetings or courses. With this level of activity, you will find you are busier than you have been—as well as more successful—and you will have to plan your days carefully. You may find that you only need one day in the field since you are no longer going on many face-to-face visits to qualify prospects. Eventually, with the increase in activity and revenue, you will merit increased secretarial support.

Organizing Your Calling Days

When your job involves the phone, and you have other things to do as well, organization is of prime importance. Organize each phone-calling day at the end of the previous phone day, say at 6:00 PM. When you come in the next morning, your files, names, numbers, and daily plan will be before you, ready to go. I've watched people waste precious minutes of their 8:30-9:00 call time looking up names and numbers which should have been at their fingertips.

Keep Records

Here's how to efficiently organize your calling days. Keep a ring binder with several tabulated areas: two areas with the five workdays, one which says "two weeks," and a tab for each month. That's a total of twenty-three tabs. As I complete calls, you either delete the names or add them to the appropriate future page for follow-up or call-back. Each new month, take the accumulated names for that month and put them in the appropriate slots under a specific day or week for follow-up as required. A daily call sheet might look like this:

Name	#	Co.	Notes	Follow-up date

When you come in in the morning, this daily phone log will be on your desk with your forty or so cold calls and twenty service and support calls already laid out for you. Initially, it will be annoying and time consuming to fill in the blanks. After all, where do you get that many names? Yellow Pages? Lead sheets? It gets easier after the second week, as you have will accumulated names of people who were not available the first time, referrals, and follow-up calls of people you have sent information to. By the end of the first month, you will barely have to look for new names at all.

Choose Whom To Call

When you are faced with a blank log, how do you decide what names to put on it for cold calls? And once you decide on a company, do you call the president? The training manager?

When faced with a blank calling log, I get creative about who might use my product or service. First I look for industries I am familiar with. Then I go outside the expected range: I peruse the Yellow Pages for industries which I am unfamiliar with but sound like they might need my service. When putting together a telephone skills course, I got creative. I called collections agencies, carpet cleaning companies, mortgage lenders, and so on. The response was better than sticking with the same companies that regularly receive calls from salespeople.

When I choose a company to call, I call the main number and speak with any receptionist, telling her who I am and what I want to accomplish. I will throw myself at her mercy to get the names of appropriate people.

> "Hi. My name is Sharon Drew Morgen and I am wondering if you could help me. I am a communications skills trainer/consultant and am wondering if there is someone in your company I might talk with about possible needs. What do you suggest?"

This will get me to the right person to start with. I use the same type of opening with each new person until I reach the correct one. But I don't initially start with the president, as that will waste lots of time. Sometimes, however, if the receptionist is not helpful (which rarely happens), I will speak with the president's secretary and ask her who I should be speaking with.

For telemarketers who are calling people at home, or for people whose product is not company-specific, the Yellow or White Pages are fine, although much-used. When you call names blindly, make certain you get into perfect voice rapport, be a bit soft and hesitant, and make sure you ask if this is the right time and right person.

> "Hello. I am calling about vacuum cleaners and am wondering if this is one of your busy times and would prefer another time to have a conversation with me?"

It's a tough job to sell to someone at home in the evenings. Your success ratio will be low, but rapport will help.

Finding The Motivation

When I offer organizational plans to sales people, I regularly hear, "Sounds great. But I won't do it."

The best motivation I know to plan regular cold-calling and follow-up days is hunger: If you want to be successful, you have to pick up the phone.

When I decided to end my "early retirement" and start another business in the United States after taking two years off, I realized I had a problem. My last seven years of work history were either in Europe (five years) or non-existent (I traveled, rested, and wrote.) I had no client referrals, no established name. But I knew how to use the phone. I put together a two-day pilot program and flier, found the Yellow Pages for two major cities, one near me, one in a city I liked, and began making cold calls to industries which I guessed might be in need of my program. I made fifty cold calls per day, five days per week for ten weeks. That amounted to twenty contacts and about three pitches per day. I ended up with three public programs of eighteen people each, *no* face-to-face meetings, and $450,000 worth of contracts for the next year following the programs.

Skill Set 11

Time management

1. Make notes on how your time schedule is apportioned now. Keep a log for a week. Note the following:

   - what time you come in daily
   - the tasks you do (write them ALL down for the week to give you a clear understanding of specifically how you spend your time)
   - your breaks (stretch, lunch, visiting)
   - any pre-organizing you do for the next day
   - what time you leave

2. Break down the above information into percentages. What percentage of your time are you:

   - in meetings
   - on the phone with problems and follow-up
   - on the phone seeking new business
   - visiting staff, colleagues, bosses
   - in the field fixing problems
   - in the field on appointments

3. What is the correlation between the percentages you come up with and the amount of new business you are bringing in? Are there any glaring problems? Anything you would like to re-examine? Reschedule?

4. If you find you would like to modify your existing schedule, try the prescribed time management system in this chapter. (See "Organizing Your Calling Days," on pg. 196.) Make modifications as your particular

environment dictates. Make sure, however, to have several segments of undisturbed phone time per week.

5. Make up a log to list and annotate the cold, referral, follow-up, and service calls you wish to make during your next calling segment. Do this on the evening before you are scheduled to make them. Note any difficulties or resistance to creating the list. Are you willing to work with your resistance or do you need to create a schedule for yourself in a different way? I recommend you create some methodology of structuring the time segment to give you maximum time usage.

6. Create some type of note-keeping or filing system for personal comments on each call. Keep these alphabetically listed with a separate place for dead cards. Once the dead cards begin to pile up, reread them to see if there are any patterns to their failure. Note if any of these names should be put on a mailing list, resurrected, or thrown away.

7. Are you noticing any personal resistance to calls? To the structure? To the schedule? What is it about? Are you having difficulties that fall into a pattern? Note the area which is giving you the resistance. What do you need to know or do to create a new choice for yourself?

8. Keep to your schedule for three weeks. What is your workload or success rate? Are you getting positive results? If not, find the problems by going through your calling patterns: call goals, time spent on each call, questioning strategies, flexibility around rapport. Are you willing to change behaviors to become more successful? Is it obvious which behaviors need modification? If not, use your tape recorder and record all conversations to note your patterns (one-way recording will give you what you need).

Conclusion

On one particular Friday, it was 5:10 and I was tired. I had made forty-nine calls and wanted to quit for the weekend. But I had promised myself fifty calls per day. I pushed myself to make the last call, assuming the sales manager would have already left. I was wrong. Here's how the call went:

Client: Hello. This had better be a good call because I'm in a rotten mood today.
SDM: Uh oh. I'm in trouble already and I don't even know you.
Client: How could you be in trouble if we don't know each other?
SDM: Because this is a *sales call.*
Client: So what are you selling?

By the time we finished speaking, the man had given me the name of the person who ran all of his sales programs and told me to tell him I was to be put into a time slot for the next month. It was a $75,000 contract. And it took a ten-minute call and one meeting.

It's do-able. There's no magic in it. The business is there. The customers are there. The needs are there. All you have to do is pick up the phone, get into relationship with the person on the other end, and you are on your way to success.

Good luck.

Author's Invitation

I am so excited by the prospect of changing the way sales are conducted in the country that I am delighted to make myself as accessible as possible to you in your discovery and change process.

I would love to hear from you: your successes and failures, trials and errors, questions and answers.

Please stay in touch with me to keep me informed. Write to me at:

Te International
P.O. Box 1318
Taos, NM 87571
(505) 776-2509

Glossary

Association: working out of and creating judgements through your personal values and personality. Operating out of Self.

Belief system: the set of standards through which each of us assess the world.

Buying environment: the space created through rapport and questioning strategies, between the buyer and seller, which gives the buyer the opportunity to explore impending resource needs which the seller can satisfy.

Buying facilitation: creating an environment of comfort through which a buyer can discover needs and negotiate the distance between the Present state and the Desired state.

Buying patterns: the historic behaviors an individual works from when deciding when, how, why, and with whom to make a purchase.

Closed questions: questions which elicit a Yes or No response.

Conscious competence: performing with excellence while being aware of your actions through internal dialogue: You "know that you know."

Conscious incompetence: performing actions with less-than-successful results while being aware of, and unable to change, the actions you are performing. You "know that you don't know."

Content: the personal and environmental specifics contained in a conversation.

Criterial rapport: matching, agreeing with, or accepting another's value system.

Disassociation: the ability to step back, describe, and report on the world through the eyes of an Observer with no attachment or judgement.

Facilitating questions: questions about the Present situation.

Filters: the set of historical ideas and judgements we see through.

Inviting questions: introductory and rapport building questions.

Language patterns: verbal decisions which are unique to an individual and include personal uses of voice, words, phrasing, definitions, emphasis, and phrasing.

Leading questions: questions phrased in a way which presuppose an answer.

Listening: a system of chosen auditory behaviors which move between Self, Other, Observer, and neutral and involves hearing content, meta-messages, and language patterns.

Maps: the unique system of values, beliefs, needs, expectations, and perceptions through which each person views the world.

Match: the mirroring of others in behavior, beliefs, values, or body language.

Meta-message: the underlying, mostly unspoken communication which is the true meaning of what is being said.

Mismatch: the accidental or deliberate rejection of meeting another's verbal or physical reality.

Observer: a state of having a perspective on your own behavior which provides opportunity for choices. Operating through disassociation.

Open questions: unstructured questions which get a response which may or may not be within the structure of the topics which need to be addressed.

Organizing questions: questions which assist in solving or examining resource problems.

Other: a state of noticing your own behavior by positioning yourself in someone else's place (through the "map" of another person).

Rapport: meeting another person, verbally or non-verbally, at his/her state of comfort through beliefs and value systems, body language, and any other point of similarity.

Self: a state of operating out of one's own belief patterns, values, or "map".

Selling patterns: the preset behaviors salespeople use in order to convince, manipulate, or otherwise influence a prospective buyer into buying what they want to sell.

Specifying questions: questions which lead from the Present situation to any Desired situation.

Summary questions: recapitulating the essence or content of another's shared information.

Unconscious competence: performing with excellence without having awareness of the components of the actions involved. You "don't know that you know."

Unconscious incompetence: performing without meeting your personal standards of excellence and being unaware that your outcome is less than satisfactory until after the fact. You "don't know that you don't know."

"We space": the unique system created when two people meld and modify their individual needs in order to be able to act and make decisions out of the relationship created between them.

Index

About The Author

Sharon Drew Morgen is an international Business Consultant specializing in sales/telephone skills training.

Early in her work history, Ms. Morgen was a PR woman, social worker, and insurance broker. After being a stockbroker for Merrill Lynch, EF Hutton, and Kidder Peabody, Ms. Morgen began a computer support services company in England in 1984 and grew it to a revenue of $5 million in four years. The company developed into a 43-person, two-country organization which specialized in supporting the technical needs in major corporations (Citibank, Xerox, Reuters American Express, British Airways, etc.). While traveling between her offices in Stuttgart, Hamburg, and London, she personally produced over 60% of the sales revenue—achieved through her ability to create and maintain loyal business relationships on the phone.

In 1984, Ms. Morgen began studying communications skills and began designing and teaching programs for her technical and sales staff to increase their ability to gather appropriate information from clients. After leaving the company in 1988, she began consulting and functioning as a business communications skills and sales consultant in Europe.

She returned to the States in 1989, and retired to Taos, New Mexico, to take a breather and gain perspective from the land. It is here she wrote her book about the blending of sales and relationship which had made her so successful in Europe. She has put it all together—the people, the business, the communication, and the spirit, into a new business paradigm: relationship-based business based on trust, respect, and integrity.

When Ms. Morgen trains, consults, or writes about sales, she works from the experience of having been a multi-million dollar producer who has created her own brand of selling: people-, rather than product-oriented.

Currently, Ms. Morgen lectures, trains, and consults in the sales and telephone skills areas for major U.S. corporations, including Bethlehem Steel, USWest Cellular, Digital Equipment Corporation, Eastman Kodak, and Sandia Labs.

Resource Guides

The processes you have learned throughout this book are summarized here, in a convenient and concise format for daily use and/or quick review.

HOW CONVERSATIONS WORK
Full text pp. 50-55

Clear Your Mind
Clear your mind completely before dialing.

Say A Matched Hello
Say "hello" by matching the voice identically.

Draw A Mental Picture
Begin to make a mental picture of the person.

Introduce Yourself
Introduce yourself by name only, and ask in a style, volume, and tempo which approximate the prospect's initial voice, if he has time to talk.

Develop The "We Space"
Turn the conversation back to the prospect

Maintain Rapport
Notice shifts in the volume and tempo of this person's voice. Shift your voice accordingly.

Address Only Specific Needs
Remember to only address that part of your service capacity which will be potentially interesting to the customer.

Follow Up
Begin to disengage from the conversation by asking the client where you should go from there.

Get A Referral
If the prospect believes you have no reason to work together, ask if he knows anyone who might be interested in your services.

Make Future Plans
Always end the call with some plans for continued collaboration.

THE STEP-BY-STEP PROCESS
Full text pp. 76-87

• Inviting Questions
• Facilitating Questions
• Specifying Questions
• Organizing Questions
and
• Differentiating Questions
• Summary Questions

WHAT NOT TO SAY AND DO
Full text pp. 165-167

• Do not use the prospect's name often
• Skip the insincere questions
• Don't impose on the client's time
• Avoid making a pitch unless the client's qualified
• Don't oversell
• Don't ask, "how are you?"
• Don't push a meeting
• Delete the sense of urgency
• Throw away methods to convince, manipulate, or close
• Don't talk, listen
• Don't criticize your competitors
• Don't leave your name
• Don't linger

LISTENING
Full text pp. 122-130

1. Minimize Internal Dialogue
Remain internally neutral.

2. The Voice
Match the person's voice and initial greeting.

3. The Opening Question
Ask a general opening, Inviting question.

4. Language Patterns
Notice the sensory-based words or characteristic language patterns.

5. Associate Into Content
Begin to listen for content from an associated place.

6. Disassociate To Summarize
Have an internal dialogue to summarize what you've understood so far.

7. Getting Into Agreement
Use your internal assessment to summarize your prospect's opening remarks.

8. Facilitating Questions To Ascertain Present State
After your initial dialogue, begin asking your client Facilitating questions.

9. Assess Your Status
Direct your attention for the first time to the meta-message.

10. Listen For Content
Listen to the content.

11. Summarize
Regularly summarize what you hear.

12. Reassess The Conversation Through The Meta-Message
Keep an internal dialogue to constantly reassess all the pieces you are working with. Understand the meta-message.

13. Keep A Check
Check if you are in criterial rapport.

14. Move Between The Call And The Caller
Disassociate in order to gather the data necessary to phrase the next question.

15. Note Internal Responses
Notice if you get tense, agitated, and associated.

16. Check Other
Check on how the customer sees you.

17. Maintain The Rapport
Keep noticing the level of rapport.

18. Interpret Data
Begin interpreting data.

19. Determine The Direction Of The Conversation
Take stock of the conversation to discern exactly where it is headed.

20. Keep Rapport Checks Following Responses
Listen to ensure that your responses to questions maintain the rapport.

21. The Close Of The Initial Call
Notice when it is time to wind down the conversation.

COLD CALLS AND REFERRAL CALLS
Full text pp. 141-157

Introduction
• Say "Hello" and give your name and a one sentence description of what you do in an easy to understand and possibly slightly provocative manner. Use an identical voice match.

• Ask if it is a good time to speak.

• Start questions immediately to get your customer engaged and thinking along the lines you would like the conversation to take.

• Don't use a script. That focuses you on a "task" and takes you out of rapport.

The Initial Pitch
• Speak solely to your client's expressed areas of interest. Use the client's needs to formulate your pitch, not your own needs of selling your product.

• Check in with your client regularly to make sure you get agreement.

• Don't speak too much, too long, or cover too much ground on the initial call, unless it is one of those rare instances when everything clicks.

• Use caution. Just because the prospect has begun initiating the questions doesn't mean you have a customer.

• Tell success stories wherever applicable.

Handling Objections
• If your prospect expresses non-acceptance or objections, listen respectfully from a disassociated place. Remember to use his buying patterns when you go back into the conversation to check and he will tell you directly what the issues are.

• When the prospect feels less than comfortable with either you or something you have said, money is the first objection.

Products Versus Services
• When selling a specific product, plan on making more cold calls to qualify, with less face-to-face contact.

• If you are calling prospects at home after hours, be respectful of their time constraints.

Ending The Initial Call
• Give the client the control over how to end your connection.

• Be prepared to visit, make a second call, send material, or any combination.

FOLLOW UP CALLS
Full text pp. 157-162

The Introduction
• Ask if the person has had a chance to look at the material you sent.

The Primary Sales Pitch
• If your customer has read your material, get agreement to have a conversation and begin asking questions.
• Highlight the specific area you will begin discussing.
• Begin to ask questions which will get your customer talking along the lines you wish to pursue.

When What You Have Isn't What They Need
• Get a referral when your product is inappropriate but you have achieved a high level of rapport.

The Close
• Let the prospect tell you how to move the sale forward, once you have agreement

Metamorphous Press

Metamorphous Press is a publisher of books and other media providing resources for personal growth and positive change. MP publishes leading-edge ideas that help people strengthen their unique talents and discover that we are responsible for our own realities.

Many of our titles center around Neurolinguistic Programming (NLP). NLP is an exciting, practical, and powerful communication model that has been able to connect observable patterns of behavior and communication and the processes that underlie them.

Metamorphous Press provides selections in many useful subject areas such as communication, health and fitness, education, business and sales, therapy, selections for young persons, and other subjects of general and specific interest. Our products are available in fine bookstores around the world.

Our distributors for North America are:

Baker & Taylor	M.A.P.S.	New Leaf
Bookpeople	Moving Books	Pacific Pipeline
Ingram		The Distributors

For those of you overseas, we are distributed by:

Airlift (UK, Western Europe)
Specialist Publications (Australia)

New selections are added regularly and availability and prices change, so call for a current catalog or to be put on our mailing list. If you have difficulty finding our products in your favorite bookstore, or if you prefer to order by mail, we will be happy to make our books and other products available to you directly. Please call or write us at:

Metamorphous Press
P.O. Box 10616   Portland, OR 97210-0616
TEL (503) 228-4972
FAX (503) 223-9117

TOLL FREE ORDERING
1-800-937-7771

METAMORPHOUS Advanced Product Services

METAMORPHOUS ADVANCED PRODUCT SERVICES (M.A.P.S.) is the master distributor for Metamorphous Press and other fine publishers.

M.A.P.S. offers books, cassettes, videos, software, and miscellaneous products in the following subjects; Bodywork, Business & Sales; Children; Education; Enneagram; Health; (including Alexander Technique and Rolfing); Hypnosis; Personal Development; Psychology (including Neurolinguistic Programming); and Relationships/Sexuality.

If you cannot find our books at your favorite bookstore, you can order directly from M.A.P.S.

TO ORDER OR REQUEST A FREE CATALOG:

MAIL   M.A.P.S.
            P.O. Box 10616
            Portland, OR 97210-0616

FAX   (503) 223-9117

CALL   Toll free 1-800-233-MAPS
                             (6277)

ALL OTHER BUSINESS:

CALL   (503) 228-4972